TEACHING WRITING
Differentiated Instruction With Leveled Graphic Organizers

NANCY L. WITHERELL & MARY C. McMACKIN

NEW YORK • TORONTO • LONDON • AUCKLAND • SYDNEY
MEXICO CITY • NEW DELHI • HONG KONG • BUENOS AIRES

Teaching
Resources

Dedication

To all the teachers and students with whom we've worked.
They have greatly influenced how we think about writing.

Acknowledgments

We'd like to express our appreciation for the support we've received from the following institutions and colleagues, which has enabled us to write this book: To the Center for Research and Teaching (CART) at Bridgewater State College, Bridgewater, Massachusetts, and to Margery Staman Miller and Mario Borunda at Lesley University for their continued encouragement.

—NLW and MCM

Editor: Sarah Longhi

Content editing by Sarah Glasscock

Cover design by Maria Lilja

Interior design by Sydney Wright

ISBN-13: 978-0-545-05901-5

ISBN-10: 0-545-05901-1

Contents

Introduction

Imagine you are invited into a first-grade classroom to observe a writing lesson on sensory details. As you enter the room, you sense the children's excitement. They're sitting in a circle on the floor and examining their teacher's jacket—a bright purple jacket covered with buttons that have slogans and photos on them and a flower sticking out of one of the pockets. The teacher has asked his students to use their senses to help them describe his jacket. He has explained that using our senses—sight, smell, touch, hearing, and taste—can help us create strong and vivid descriptions. This scenario introduces the interactive lesson the teacher has prepared to teach this concept. He continues by engaging students in a read-aloud of a picture book; he stops often to ask children to describe what the characters might be seeing, smelling, feeling, and so on. Then he displays a picture and models how he would use his senses to describe the people, objects, and actions in it. In the next phase of the lesson, children move on to visualizing a scene and then creating a chart of words and actions to describe it. At the end of the lesson, they are ready to work independently on describing with sensory details.

The teacher passes out a graphic organizer to each student. Once the students begin to work, you notice that all the organizers look equally demanding but that there are slight differences in what the children are doing. All of them are completing charts to help them write descriptions, but the charts vary from simple to complex. Some students are drawing a picture and writing sensory details to describe it, some are drawing a picture and using adjectives and actions to describe it, and some are visualizing an object or scene to describe with sensory details. You realize that this teacher is using tiered (leveled) graphic organizers to differentiate writing instruction.

Differentiated Instruction

Tomlinson (1999) explains that teachers can modify three basic areas: content, process, and product. When we differentiate by using leveled graphic organizers, we are modifying products.

We know that when we introduce a skill to a whole class (or even a subset of a class), the children in the group are not likely to learn at the same rate. Some will catch on to the skill faster than others, and some will be able to demonstrate their understanding in more complex ways than others. In order for all children to learn at an optimal pace, we match them with a reinforcing activity that allows each one to be successful at a cognitively appropriate level. A teacher, for example, provides whole-class instruction on all-about books, small nonfiction books that focus on one topic. After a lesson in which the teacher models this concept using the book *Koalas* by Gail Saunders-Smith (1997), students work independently on an activity that will help them reinforce and extend what they've learned. Several students work on beginning graphic organizers in which they draw pictures of the topic they want to work on. Several other students work on graphic organizers similar in content to the beginning organizer, but this developing organizer also includes a table of contents. The remaining students work on a slightly more complex graphic organizer where they add a small glossary that lists three or four important words and what each means.

At all three levels, students are using graphic organizers to reinforce the concept of all-about books that the teacher introduced to the entire group. Each student feels successful because he or she is matched to an appropriate graphic organizer—one that is neither too easy nor too difficult.

Why Use Tiered Graphic Organizers?

In order to meet the diverse needs of students in today's classrooms, teachers must be able to design lessons that (1) meet individual instructional requirements, (2) stay within what is often mandated curriculum, and (3) ensure consistent outcomes for all students. The use of tiered graphic organizers can help us achieve our instructional goals.

We have created organizers on three levels: a *beginning* level where students demonstrate a basic understanding of the target concept using pictures and a limited amount of writing; a *developing* level that is applicable for students who are ready to engage, with some support, in higher levels of thinking and writing; and an *extended* level that is appropriate for students who are able to work, with limited support, on material that is more cognitively advanced than the lower two levels. Leveled graphic organizers make it possible for teachers to match each student with developmentally appropriate comprehension activities while

focusing on one overarching outcome for all students.

Although each graphic organizer fosters a different type and amount of thinking, the organizers look equally demanding and appealing. It's important to note that graphic organizers are not end products; rather, they are planners that students use to record ideas for a subsequent activity. In the primary grades, students might work on individual organizers and then share their ideas orally in a whole-class discussion. Other times, students might use the organizers as planning tools for writing activities. In all cases, the organizers should be viewed as a means to an end, not a final product.

Building Concepts for Primary Students

When we teach writing, we address the developmental needs and interests of primary grade children. We also emphasize the need to build (as opposed to reinforce) concepts. Acquiring a thorough understanding of literary concepts in the primary grades is extremely crucial because this understanding forms the foundation for a deeper development of these same concepts in the intermediate grades and beyond. Most three-, four-, and five-year-olds have already begun to construct knowledge and understanding about writing—where, when, why, and how it's used (Rowe, 2008). We built on this research and our own experiences as we created the lessons and tiered graphic organizers to accompany the 15 concepts in this book. We encourage you to reinforce the concepts in practical ways throughout the school year.

How Is This Book Organized?

Each chapter follows the same organizational structure:

- Name and define a target concept

- Provide an activity through which we introduce the concept to students

- Transition from a concrete activity to a piece of quality literature to illustrate the concept in a more abstract form

- Offer a model lesson in which we provide direct instruction of the concept that prepares students for the tiered graphic organizers

- Include three tiered graphic organizers: beginning, developing, and extended

- List two picture books and one chapter book, with annotations, that teachers can use in a follow-up lesson

Is This a Workbook?

No. It is not our intent to offer a "writing workbook," even though workbooks can be useful for some students. Our goal is to help students prepare to write. Workbooks are texts that can be used one time—once the answers have been recorded on a page, the workbook has served its purpose. Conversely, the activities in this book are open-ended and may be used over and over again as your students continue to grow and develop.

◆ ◆ ◆

You can use the chapters in *Teaching Writing: Differentiated Instruction With Leveled Graphic Organizers* as stand-alone chapters or as units of study that build on one another. We do recommend that some chapters be taught before others; for example, the chapter on

book reports should be taught after the chapters on character and plot. In addition, the lessons and activities in this book can easily be incorporated into any language arts curriculum.

We created the tiered graphic organizers in this book to help you meet the needs of all learners as they continue to grow as writers over time. Watching children flourish as writers is exciting, but it takes focused work and an understanding on the part of the teacher of what each child can do on any given day. We hope you find differentiating learning with tiered graphic organizers to be a useful tool in your classroom.

Sources Cited

Rowe, D. W. (2008). Social contracts for writing: Negotiating shared understandings about text in the preschool years. *Reading Research Quarterly, 43*(1), 68–95.

Tomlinson, C. A. (1999). *The differentiated classroom: Responding to the needs of all learners.* Alexandria, VA: ASCD.

Describing With Sensory Details

Skill: *Write a clear description of an object.*

Description

Writers want a reader to "see" what is in their mind as they write. To do this, they add descriptions to enhance these images. Writers use adjectives to translate their sensory impressions into words. They "paint a picture" with their words so readers will be able to visualize the experience, too. Our goal is to have children write description that makes a text come alive.

Getting to Know the Concept

Introduce this concept by walking into class carrying a flamboyant purse or wearing an outrageous jacket. After grouping children in a circle so everyone can see, display the item and then pass it around for students to inspect. Ask children to describe the item and write down the words and phrases they use on chart paper. Encourage them to focus on the five senses—seeing, hearing, tasting, smelling, feeling—and to be as creative as possible. To spark new ideas and generate additional words and phrases, insert your own observations, too. Talk about how you studied the item carefully so you could describe it with specific words to show how it looked, felt, sounded, and smelled.

Teaching the Concept With Literature

Often descriptions in texts are interspersed with dialogue or the plot, but if you scour your collections, you're likely to find wonderful examples of descriptive writing. We look for short, explicit descriptions, such as those in *Angelina at the Palace* (Holabird, 2005) that describe the countryside surrounding the palace or the princesses at a dinner Angelina attended. Use the pictures in this book and in others to have students describe which senses the characters are experiencing. What can the characters in the picture see, hear, smell, taste, or feel?

Model Lesson

Begin by telling students that an adjective describes a noun or pronoun and gives information about the word it describes. For instance, we might say we see a *little* dog.

The word *little* signals that it is not a German shepherd. Ask students what kind of dog they picture when they hear the words *little dog*.

Then review the five senses—sight, hearing, touch, smell, and taste—and begin writing a list of adjectives that are related to the senses, such as *gigantic, purple, noisy, crackling, soft, furry, dusty,* and *sour*. Let students tell you which sense each adjective is related to. Then encourage them to suggest other adjectives, or describing words, for the list.

After finishing the list, create a four-column chart on the board like the one shown at the bottom of the page. Display a picture that shows people or animals engaged in an activity. On the chart, model words you could use to describe what you would see, hear, smell, taste, or feel if you were in the picture. For example, if the picture you chose shows people enjoying a day at the beach, your chart might look like the one below.

As the example shows, it may not always be possible to include a word or phrase in the last column. If necessary, point this out to students. When you have several ideas for each sense, show how you can write a description by putting together everything you see, then everything you hear, and so forth: *We see decorated sand castles, and a jumping dog playing Frisbee. We hear excited children yelling to each other.*

Finally, display a blank copy of the chart. Ask students to think of an object or a scene to describe. Rather than working with an illustration, this time they will visualize what they are describing. Demonstrate how you would use adjectives to describe an event by thinking about what you would hear, see, smell, feel, and taste. Once you have completed several rows of the chart, model how you would use these notes to write a description of the event. Emphasize that you tried to use precise words to create a clear picture for your readers.

Graphic Organizers

When students understand that they can create clearer descriptions by including the five senses, they are ready to complete one of the sensory detail organizers. You might suggest the following objects or scenes for students to describe: a slice of watermelon or a dill pickle, a snowball, being in a toy store, eating lunch in the cafeteria, visiting a friend's home.

Sense	Adjective (describing word)	What is being described?	What is the person or thing doing?
see	decorated	sand castles	
see	a jumping	dog	playing Frisbee
hear	excited	children	yelling to each other
feel	bright hot	sun	making shadows with the beach umbrellas
smell	spicy	salsa	slipping off corn chips

Beginning: **Use All Your Senses**

Students draw a picture of an object or a scene with as many details as possible. Then they record what they see in their pictures, noting colors and other sensory details. Finally, students write a description of their picture.

Developing: **Sensing the Scene**

Students draw a picture of an object or scene with as many details as possible. They provide an adjective for each object and a descriptive action based on a sense. On a new sheet of paper, students write a description of their picture. Note: Students may not have entries for each row in the chart.

Extending: **Making Sense of Details**

Students identify the object or scene they want to describe. They use each of the five senses to think of an adjective and elaborate by including another detail and/or a descriptive action. Then they write a description of the object or scene.

Great Books for This Activity

Picture Books

Holabird, K. (2005). *Angelina at the palace.* New York: Viking.

Steig, W. (1986). *Brave Irene.* New York: Farrar, Straus and Giroux. (See the section when Irene first spots the palace or when she attends the ball.)

Wong, J. S. (2000). *The trip back home.* San Diego, CA: Harcourt. (See the description of the gifts the girl and her mother take to Korea.)

Chapter Book

Adler, D. A. (1984). *Cam Jansen and the mystery of the monster movie.* New York: Yearling. (See the last paragraph on page 9.)

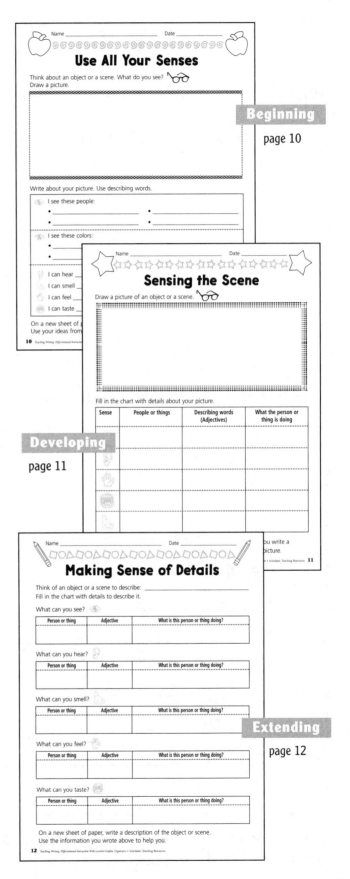

Beginning
page 10

Developing
page 11

Extending
page 12

Name _____ Date _____

Use All Your Senses

Think about an object or a scene. What do you see?
Draw a picture.

Write about your picture. Use describing words.

I see these people:

- _____   • _____
- _____   • _____

I see these colors:

- _____   • _____
- _____   • _____

I can hear _____

I can smell _____

I can feel _____

I can taste _____

On a new sheet of paper, write a description of your picture.
Use your ideas from above.

Sensing the Scene

Draw a picture of an object or a scene.

Fill in the chart with details about your picture.

Sense	People or things	Describing words (Adjectives)	What the person or thing is doing
(eye)			
(ear)			
(hand)			
(mouth)			
(nose)			

Choose three or more details from your chart. Use them to help you write a description. On a new sheet of paper, write a description of your picture.

Name _____ Date _____

Making Sense of Details

Think of an object or a scene to describe: _____

Fill in the chart with details to describe it.

What can you see?

Person or thing	Adjective	What is this person or thing doing?

What can you hear?

Person or thing	Adjective	What is this person or thing doing?

What can you smell?

Person or thing	Adjective	What is this person or thing doing?

What can you feel?

Person or thing	Adjective	What is this person or thing doing?

What can you taste?

Person or thing	Adjective	What is this person or thing doing?

On a new sheet of paper, write a description of the object or scene.
Use the information you wrote above to help you.

Elaborating: Expanding a Simple Idea

Skill: *Build upon an idea to make it clearer.*

Description

It's typical for a beginning writer to draw a picture and then write a sentence to go with the picture. The child writes his or her part of a conversational exchange and stops. Linguists often refer to this one statement as a conversational turn. Our goal is to have students expand an idea (elaborate) by anticipating what the reader might want or need to know—and continue the exchange in writing. To help in expanding an idea, we begin by focusing on the five W's (Who, What, When, Where, Why) + How.

Getting to Know the Concept

We suggest you introduce this concept by providing a straightforward, basic account of an exciting piece of information, in essence, sharing what a beginning writer might record in a conversational turn. For example, you might say, "I got a new puppy." Stop and ask students if there is anything else they'd like to know about the puppy. They will likely pose questions such as "What kind of puppy?" "What's the puppy's name?" "Why did you name him Dustmop?" "How old is he?" "Where does he sleep?" "When will you bring him to school so we can see him?" "Who takes Dustmop for walks?"

Record children's questions and then categorize them into the five W's + How. If students ask a question such as "Is his fur soft?" record it; when sorting this question into the five W's + How, note that this question is really asking how the puppy feels. Students should begin to recognize that they can build on their initial ideas by asking themselves who, what, where, when, why, and how questions.

Teaching the Concept With Literature

To teach children to elaborate on simple ideas, look for books with simple ideas that are clearly developed. On almost every page of *Gilberto and the Wind* (Ets, 1978), the author begins with a sentence that could serve as a conversational turn and then adds another sentence or two to elaborate on the original idea. When discussing the author's words, discuss whether he is telling who, what, when, where, why, or how. On one page, for example, Ets writes that the wind loves to play with laundry drying on an outside clothesline. By itself, this sentence would match the illustration and move the story forward. However, in the following sentences, Ets builds on it by describing how the wind turns pillowcases into balloons, blows sheets and apron strings, and pulls out clothespins.

Model Lesson

We suggest that you read *Wemberly Worried* (Henkes, 2000) for pleasure and then return to it to examine how Henkes elaborates on several of his ideas. The book begins with one sentence that reveals that Wemberly, a small mouse, worries about everything. Write the first sentence of the book across the top of a piece of chart paper and then continue to read the book aloud. The following pages and illustrations explain what Wemberly worries about, when she worries, and where she worries. Below the sentence you wrote, create a six-column chart labeled "Who," "What," "Where," "When," "Why," and "How." Record each detail in the appropriate column. The top of your chart might look like the chart below.

Next, return to the first page of the book and explain that good authors do more than write a short sentence to go with each detailed picture in their books. They do what Henkes does. They add more to a sentence or add more sentences to give the reader more information. Authors tell us the who, what, when, where, why, and how of the story, and that's what makes the story interesting!

After students have explored *Wemberly Worried*, write the following sentence on a dry erase board: "My sister's tooth fell out." Model some examples of "who" questions someone might ask to learn more about this event—for instance, "Who did your sister tell about her tooth?" Think of an interesting answer for your question and model how you would write your response to it.

Then, divide the class into six groups and give each group a job. One group will elaborate on this sentence by brainstorming additional Who questions and then writing an answer to its favorite one. The second group will brainstorm What questions and write an answer to its favorite one. Assign Where, When, Why, and How to the remaining groups.

When each group has completed the brainstorming work, have one child from the group share its most interesting question. Write the question under the target sentence on the board and label it "Who," "What," "Where," "When," "Why," or "How."

My sister's tooth fell out.

Q: Who told her how to get it to fall out?

Then have the child read the target sentence and record the answer to the question they posed, for instance:

My sister's tooth fell out. My big brother, Jim, told her to crunch down on an apple to make it fall out.

Conclude by pointing out that students can use question words to trigger new ideas when they write.

Who	What	Where	When	Why	How
It seems like she's worried about her parents, but she's really worried about herself.	spilled juice shrinking while taking a bath		morning, night, all day		

Graphic Organizers

When students can use question words to expand simple ideas, they are ready for one of these graphic organizers. You may give a prompt to get them started such as "Tell me about your favorite toy." or "What did you do at recess?"

Beginning: **Blast Off for More**

Students draw a picture, write a sentence about it, and then add one more sentence telling more about who is in the picture or what is happening.

Developing: **Give Me Some Lip**

Students write an initial sentence, pick two question words and brainstorm possible questions. They write a sentence to answer the more interesting question.

Extending: **Go Tell It on the Mountain**

Students write an initial sentence and elaborate on it by writing three questions. They use the answers to these questions to write an elaborated sentence.

Great Books for This Activity

Picture Books

Ets, M. H. (1978). *Gilberto and the wind.* New York: Puffin.

Henkes, K. (1995). *Good-bye, Curtis.* New York: Greenwillow. (See the first page which tells why this is an important day for Curtis.)

Henkes, K. (2000). *Wemberly worried.* New York: Greenwillow.

Wells, R. (2000). *Emily's first 100 days of school.* New York: Hyperion. (Starting on the first page, Emily elaborates on how she feels and what happens in school.)

Chapter Book

Lowry, L. (2002). *Gooney Bird Greene.* Boston: Houghton Mifflin. (The first paragraph describes when Gooney Bird arrives at her new school and what she is wearing).

Name _____ Date _____

Blast Off for More

Draw a picture in the top
of the spaceship.

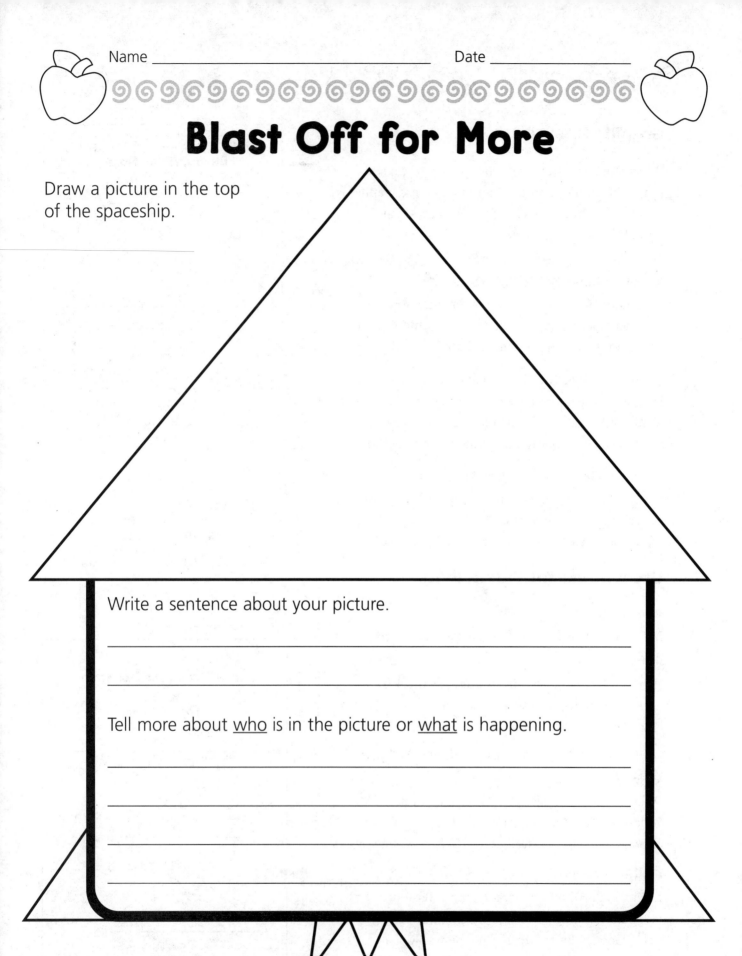

Write a sentence about your picture.

_____

_____

Tell more about <u>who</u> is in the picture or <u>what</u> is happening.

_____

_____

_____

_____

Give Me Some Lip

Write a sentence.

_____
_____

Think more about your sentence. Circle two words.

WHO?	WHEN?	WHY?
WHAT?	WHERE?	HOW?

Write a question for each question word you circled.

1. _____
_____

2. _____
_____

Write a new sentence that answers one of your questions.

_____
_____

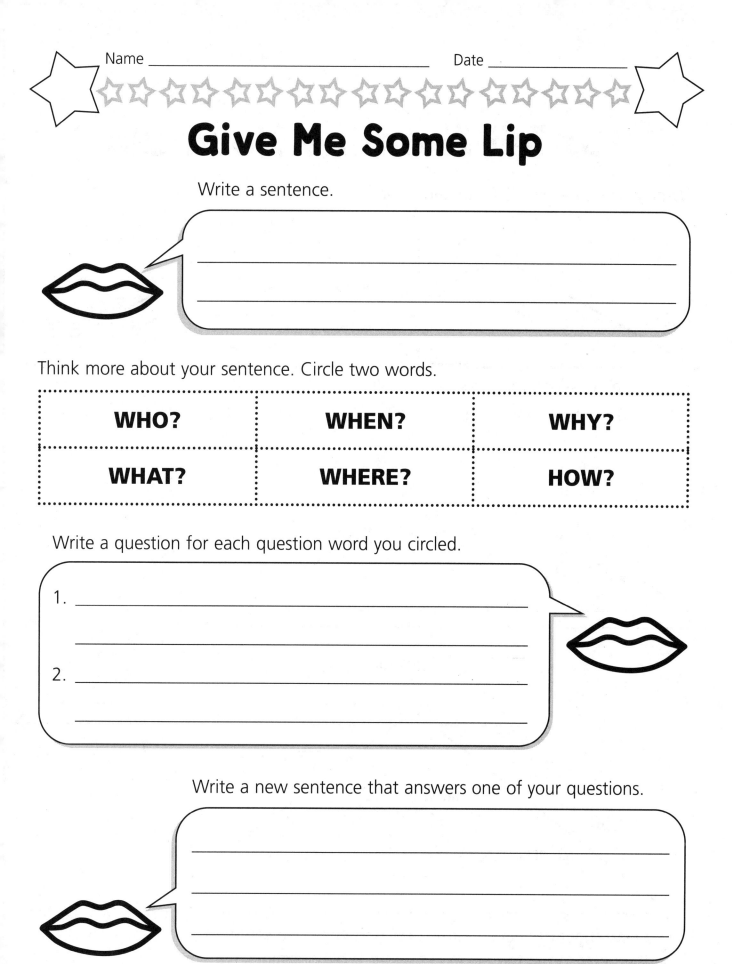

Go Tell It on the Mountain

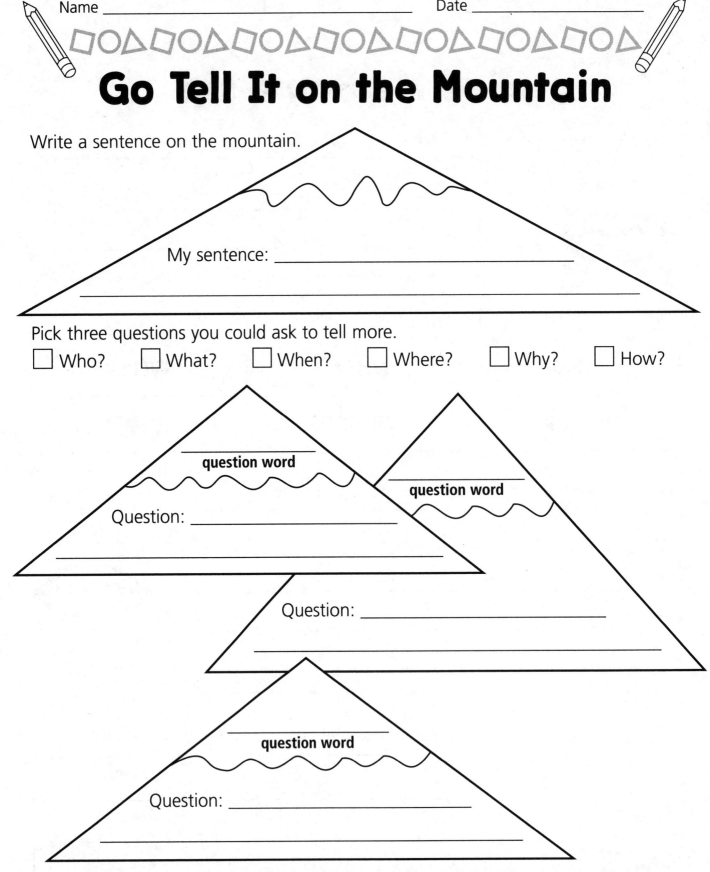

Write a sentence on the mountain.

My sentence: _____

_____

Pick three questions you could ask to tell more.

☐ Who?   ☐ What?   ☐ When?   ☐ Where?   ☐ Why?   ☐ How?

_____
question word

Question: _____

_____

_____
question word

Question: _____

_____

_____
question word

Question: _____

_____

On a new sheet of paper, write a new and improved sentence.
Use the details from the answers to your three questions.

Showing, Not Telling

Skill: *Reveal information rather than expressing it directly.*

Description

Young children tend to have vivid imaginations. They tell elaborate oral stories replete with details that help listeners create pictures in their minds. When they write, however, they often compress their ideas into a few underdeveloped sentences. Often, the sentences resemble lists of semi-related ideas. To help children engage their readers, we teach them to show what's happening and how their characters are feeling, rather than telling readers about their subjects. For example, instead of telling that a character was scared of spiders, a writer might say that the character jumped a mile every time she saw a spider and ran screaming to her mom for help.

Getting to Know the Concept

To begin this process of showing rather than telling, we suggest you use a variation of a charades-like game. Ask a student volunteer to act out a command you've written on a sentence strip or whispered into his or her ear. For instance, you might suggest that the student pretend to be bored, to have a cold, or to search for a lost pencil. When the other children guess the action, talk about what the volunteer did that was effective and question whether he or she could have done anything else to reveal the action. Point out that you could have just told everyone what was written on your sentence strip, but that it was more interesting for everyone to figure out the action. Note, too, that it was more fun for the volunteer to think about how to show the action. Explain that the same holds true for writers—they can tell how a character is feeling or what is happening, but it's more fun for readers if the information is shown rather than told.

Teaching the Concept With Literature

Picture books by nature tend to *tell*, while the supporting illustrations *show* information. You may have to look through your collection to find exemplars for Show, Don't Tell, but there are many wonderful books to use, such as *Will's New Cap* (Landstrom & Landstrom, 1992). In this book, instead of saying that Will scraped his knee when he tripped, the authors say, "Ouch!" "Blood!" "Will limps all the way home." Because the authors show rather than tell what Will is experiencing, we can feel Will's discomfort on each page

Model Lesson

The picture book *Nine for California* (Levitin, 1996) contains many examples of Show, Don't Tell. After you read this book, or another text, aloud for enjoyment, go back and talk about the details the illustrator included in the pictures. To prepare students for the Beginning graphic organizer, select one picture and have them brainstorm as many details as they can find. Explain that illustrators and writers show information to help readers feel as if they are experiencing what the characters are experiencing.

Next, create a two-column T-chart like the one shown below. As you reread *Nine for California* aloud, stop every time the author shows something about the characters, the situations in which they find themselves, or the setting. In the left column of the chart, record the words the author uses to reveal, or show, information. Then, using a think-aloud, model what these words show, and record your thinking in the right column of the chart. Your chart might look like the one below.

After identifying and discussing how the author uses dialogue and descriptions to show, rather than tell, have students create their own examples. Provide a situation for students to consider (e.g., Sam was upset when he got to school because he left his lunch on the school bus), write it in the right column of a T-chart, and have students determine what details they would use to show this scene. Encourage them to use both dialogue and descriptive language. Record their responses in the left column. Finally, give pairs of students a simple sentence (e.g., My cat is smart) and have them write a description that would show, rather than tell, this information. Conclude by bringing students together, having them read their descriptions, and discussing what made their descriptions effective examples.

Graphic Organizers

When students can reveal information by showing, rather than telling, they are ready for one of the graphic organizers. You may suggest one of these ideas for students to describe: a character is afraid of the dark or is thirsty, a baby is a messy eater, a child is lost, it's hot outside, or a little girl's favorite color is purple.

Words in the Book That Show	What Do the Words Show?
We all sat so close that our knees knocked.	All nine characters are jammed into a tight space.
my tummy felt funny, beans and prunes acting up	Amanda felt sick.
Miss Camilla's face got very red. "Children should be seen and not heard," she said.	She was angry because the children were too noisy.

Beginning: **Picture Show**

Students draw a detailed picture and then list what their picture shows.

Developing: **Show Time**

Students identify what they want to show. They generate two ideas for ways to show (not tell) about their idea. Then they show rather than tell about their subject in a written description.

Extending: **Show Me!**

Students identify what they want to show, list actions and lines of dialogue they might hear that describe the subject vividly, and then include both in a description.

Great Books for This Activity

Picture Books

Carlson, N. (1999). *Look out kindergarten, here I come!* New York: Viking. (See the second page where the author shows that Henry is excited.)

Henkes, K. (1989). *Jessica.* New York: Greenwillow. (See the first few pages where the author shows that Ruthie is lonely so she invents Jessica, an invisible friend.)

Landstrom, O., & Landstrom, L. (1992). *Will's new cap.* New York: Farrar, Straus and Giroux.

Levitin, S. (1996). *Nine for California.* New York: Orchard.

Chapter Book

Giff, P .R. (1997). *Starring Rosie* (Ballet Slippers series). New York: Viking. (See page 2 where the author shows that Andrew is sad.)

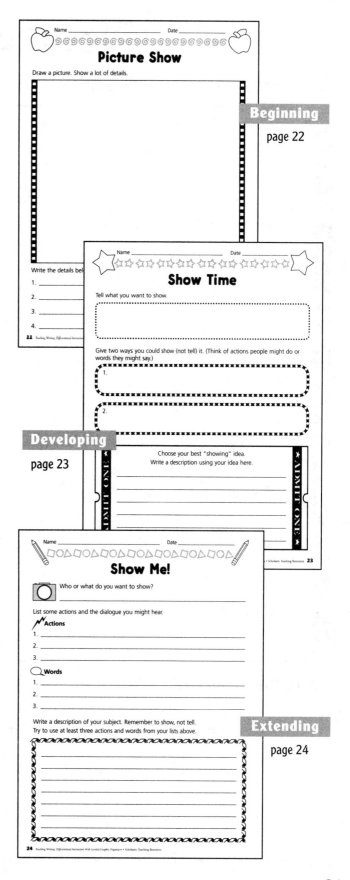

Picture Show

Draw a picture. Show a lot of details.

Write the details below.
1. _____
2. _____
3. _____
4. _____

Beginning
page 22

Show Time

Tell what you want to show.

Give two ways you could show (not tell) it. (Think of actions people might do or words they might say.)
1.
2.

Choose your best "showing" idea.
Write a description using your idea here.

Developing
page 23

Show Me!

Who or what do you want to show?

List some actions and the dialogue you might hear.
Actions
1. _____
2. _____
3. _____

Words
1. _____
2. _____
3. _____

Write a description of your subject. Remember to show, not tell.
Try to use at least three actions and words from your lists above.

Extending
page 24

Name _____ Date _____

Picture Show

Draw a picture. Show a lot of details.

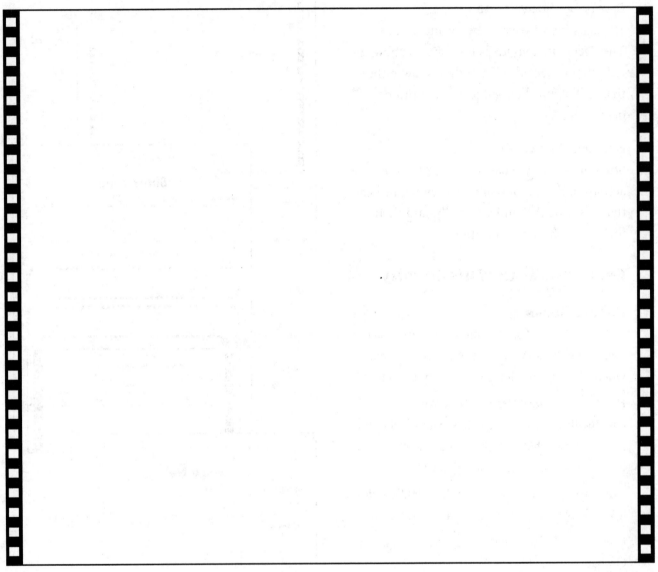

Write the details below.

1. _____

2. _____

3. _____

4. _____

 Teaching Writing: Differentiated Instruction With Leveled Graphic Organizers • Scholastic Teaching Resources

Show Time

Tell what you want to show.

Give two ways you could show (not tell) it. (Think of actions people might do or words they might say.)

1.

2.

Choose your best "showing" idea.
Write a description using your idea here.

ADMIT ONE

ADMIT ONE

_____
_____
_____
_____
_____
_____

Name _____   Date _____

Show Me!

Who or what do you want to show?

_____

List some actions and the dialogue you might hear.

Actions

1. _____

2. _____

3. _____

Words

1. _____

2. _____

3. _____

Write a description of your subject. Remember to show, not tell.
Try to use at least three actions and words from your lists above.

_____

_____

_____

_____

_____

_____

_____

Writing a Paragraph

Skill: *Write a series of related sentences about one topic.*

Description

A paragraph is a well-organized set of sentences about one topic. In the primary grades, instruction begins with simple three-sentence paragraphs that contain a beginning, middle, and end. As students move through the primary grades, we want them to write each paragraph with a topic sentence that lets the reader know what the paragraph is about, several sentences in which they elaborate on the main idea, and a conclusion. Indentation is also introduced in the primary grades as a signal that writers use to let readers know they are switching to a new topic.

Getting to Know the Concept

In order to make the concept of a paragraph more concrete, you might want to use the following bicycle analogy, which we'll continue to build on in the model lesson. Enlarge a simple drawing of a person riding a bike and explain that a bicycle has three basic parts: the first part (front wheel and handlebars), the middle part (seat and pedals) and the last part (back wheel and brake). Let students know that a paragraph has three parts, too: the first part, the middle part, and the last part. To illustrate this point, write a simple paragraph on chart paper, such as the following:

> *On Saturday, I scored my first goal in soccer. Timmy kicked the ball to me, and I kicked it with all my might. It went right past the goalie and into the net.*

After reading the paragraph aloud to the class, reread each sentence, associating it with the corresponding part of the bike. Point to the indentation at the beginning of the paragraph and remind students that we indent to show readers that we are starting a new paragraph and switching to a new topic.

Teaching the Concept With Literature

Since picture books often contain limited text or are written in justified (block) alignment, you may have to check several books to find an indented paragraph with three or four sentences about one topic to use as a model. Your best bet may be to create your own paragraph: *We just moved to a new apartment. I need to find a good place to put the music box my aunt gave me last year for my birthday. It will take me a while to get used to living in our new place.*

Model Lesson

Build on the simple bike analogy by pointing to the front tire and handlebars and saying,

"When people ride bikes, they use the front tire and handlebars to steer them in the right direction. The handlebars and front wheel point them where they want to go." Stop to let children share a few experiences they've had steering bikes and then continue: "The first sentence in a paragraph is very similar to the front wheel and handlebars of a bike; it tells one important thing about the paragraph so readers know where the paragraph is going."

Next, read aloud the following paragraph or a similar one that you've written on chart paper ahead of time: "The boy and his dog are always together. They play together after school and even sleep in the same room. The two of them are best friends."

Ask a student to reread the first sentence and discuss the important idea it conveys (the closeness of a boy and his dog). Note that this sentence lets us know where the paragraph is heading.

Then point to the middle of the bike and say, "People who ride bikes use the seat and the pedals in the middle to do most of the work; writers do most of their work in the middle of paragraphs by adding information (details) about the first sentence. Like short and long bike rides, some paragraphs are short with a few details; others are long, with many details." Talk about the information given in the middle of the paragraph.

Finally, point to the back of the bike and explain, "The brake is on the back tire. It helps you stop the bike." Again, compare the bike to a paragraph, saying, "The last sentence of a paragraph lets readers know that the paragraph is coming to an end. It tells one thing you want readers to remember." Talk about the information given in the end of the paragraph.

The chart below can be used to relate each part of the model paragraph to the bike. To reinforce this bike analogy, model how you would write a three-sentence paragraph based on a picture. Record your work on an enlarged copy of the Braking for Paragraphs graphic organizer. Then, using notes on the organizer, model how to write a descriptive paragraph and how to indent the first sentence. Finally, reread your paragraph and demonstrate how you could add another sentence to the middle of it. The sentence should tell more about the idea in the first sentence. Conclude by reviewing the three basic parts of a paragraph and reminding students that they can make paragraphs longer by adding relevant details to the middle.

Graphic Organizers

When students can focus three sentences on one narrow topic, such as finding a ten-dollar bill on the sidewalk, riding a bike down a big hill, or playing baseball with a cousin, they are

Beginning (front tire and handlebars)	Middle (driver, seat, and pedals)	End (brake and back tire)
The first sentence tells the one important thing your paragraph is about. It tells where you're going.	The middle is where you do most of the work, adding details about your topic.	The last sentence lets readers know what you want them to remember. It is like a brake. With it, your paragraph comes to a stop.

ready to complete one of the following graphic organizers.

Beginning: **Braking for Paragraphs**

Students draw a picture, tell what their picture is about (beginning), add a detail about an important part of the picture (middle), and tell what they want the reader to remember (end). They use these notes to write a three-sentence paragraph.

Developing: **A Handlebar Grip on Paragraphs**

Students draw a picture, tell what their picture is about, provide details about two important parts of the picture, and tell what they want the reader to remember to bring closure to the paragraph. They write a four-sentence paragraph that is indented.

Extending: **Cycling Into Paragraphs**

Students determine a topic for a paragraph, write an idea for a topic sentence (beginning), provide three details to tell more (middle), and include what they want the reader to remember (closure). They use their notes to write a five-sentence paragraph that is indented.

Great Books for This Activity

Picture Books

George, J. C. (1997). *Look to the north: A wolf pup diary*. New York: HarperCollins. (See the first paragraph, "7 Weeks Old.")

Old, W. (2002). *To fly: The story of the Wright brothers*. New York: Clarion. (See the sixth paragraph, page 7.)

Chapter Book

Byars, B. (1996). *Tornado*. New York: Scholastic. (See the last paragraph, page 6 or the second paragraph, page 7.)

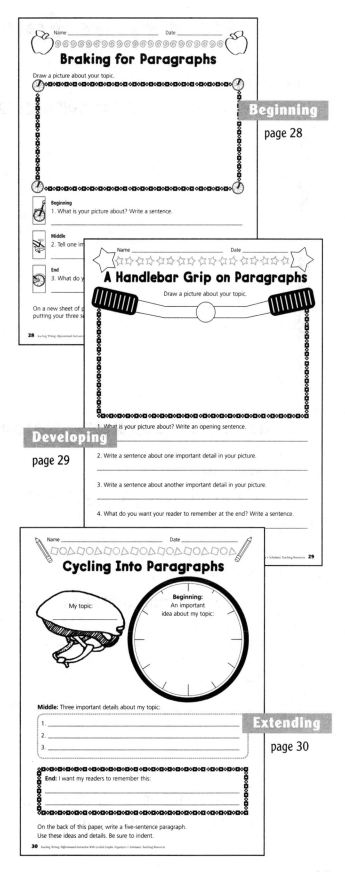

Braking for Paragraphs

Draw a picture about your topic.

Beginning

1. What is your picture about? Write a sentence.

_____

Middle

2. Tell one important detail about your picture. Write a sentence.

_____

End

3. What do you want your reader to remember? Write a sentence.

_____

On a new sheet of paper, write a paragraph by putting your three sentences together: 1 + 2 + 3.

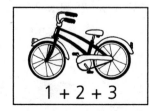

1 + 2 + 3

A Handlebar Grip on Paragraphs

Draw a picture about your topic.

1. What is your picture about? Write an opening sentence.

_____

2. Write a sentence about one important detail in your picture.

_____

3. Write a sentence about another important detail in your picture.

_____

4. What do you want your reader to remember at the end? Write a sentence.

_____

Write a four-sentence paragraph on a new sheet of paper.
Use the ideas and details from your picture. Be sure to indent!

Cycling Into Paragraphs

My topic:

_____

Beginning:
An important
idea about my topic:

Middle: Three important details about my topic:

1. _____

2. _____

3. _____

End: I want my readers to remember this:

_____

_____

On the back of this paper, write a five-sentence paragraph.
Use these ideas and details. Be sure to indent.

Writing Facts That Fascinate

Skill: *Write a factual account in an engaging voice.*

Description

As you listen to your students enter the room each morning during share time, or at recess, you probably hear them exchanging information about dinosaurs, a sports team, or a place—perhaps even a foreign country where they were born. They often discuss nonfiction topics in their oral language. Our goal in this chapter is to prepare students to write nonfiction texts. We want them to know that informational writing is based on facts rather than opinions and that informational texts do not simply list dull facts but contain carefully selected details that are written in a way that's informative and engaging.

Getting to Know the Concept

Begin by focusing on the difference between facts and opinions. Explain that a fact is something that is true. We can often find evidence to show that it's true. You might cite a fact about a child in your class, for example: "It's a fact that Luis is six years old. I know this is true. We could check by asking Luis's mom or even check his birth certificate to make sure this information is true." Explain that an opinion, on the other hand, is a belief that may or may not be true and that people can have different opinions about the same topic. Use an example about the same child to illustrate an opinion: "Some people might think that Luis tells funny jokes. That would be their opinion." After sharing a few additional examples, give a blank sheet of paper to each child. On one side of the sheet, have students write FACT in large letters. On the other side, have them write OPINION in large letters. As you read each of the statements below, students determine whether it is a fact or an opinion, and hold up the correct word on their paper to indicate their answer. (You could also do this with thumbs up and thumbs down).

- There are 60 minutes in an hour. (fact)
- Bagels are the best food for breakfast. (opinion)
- Mosquitoes bite people. (fact)
- Mosquitoes are larger than birds. (not true; therefore, not a fact)
- Mosquito bites are the worst kind of bug bites. (opinion)

We know that differentiating between fact and opinion may be difficult for primary grade children, so we don't expect perfection. The idea is to introduce students to the concept that some nonfiction writing, such as informational writing, is based exclusively on true ideas that can be verified.

Teaching the Concept With Literature

So often, when children write informational texts, their work resembles lists of lackluster facts. In order to help them become aware that each piece of informational writing should have a strong voice behind it, read aloud exemplars from this genre and point out that informational writing should not sound like an excerpt from an encyclopedia. Jerry Pallotta, a popular author of alphabet books, writes with a clear, engaging voice that young children enjoy. Each alphabetic entry consists of four or five short sentences, so they serve as ideal exemplars for primary grade children.

Model Lesson

First, review the definitions of *fact* and *opinion*. Over the next two or three days, we recommend that you read several of Jerry Pallotta's alphabet books. We'll use *The Bird Alphabet Book* for this model lesson. After reading to appreciate the information in each book, think aloud to repeat some of the facts from the book and record them in the left column of a chart like the one shown below. When that column is complete, read each item and talk about how this is a list of basic facts. Reread the sentences Pallotta uses in the book to investigate how he uses voice—how he makes his facts interesting to read. Record Pallotta's words in the right column. Your chart might look like the one below.

After analyzing *The Bird Alphabet Book* (or better still, several of Pallotta's alphabet books), select a topic that's of interest to your students (or choose one from a social studies or science topic you are studying). As a class, brainstorm facts about the topic and record the facts on a chart like the one shown below. Then rewrite the facts; make them more interesting by adding information and writing in an engaging voice.

Conclude by discussing how writers have fun making facts come alive and how readers enjoy texts that contain interesting facts. Invite children as they read independently to be on the lookout for examples of facts that have come to life.

Graphic Organizers

When students can distinguish between fact and opinion and add details that enhance voice, they are ready for one of the graphic organizers. They may be gathering facts about an animal; a local or national place of interest; a person including a family member, a notable local citizen, or an historical figure; a thing, such as a country; or a historic or current event.

Fact	How Pallotta Writes About This Fact
A bat is not a bird.	"Hey, wait a second! Bats are not birds. Bats are mammals."
The crocodile bird eats food off of other animals' teeth.	"[Crocodile birds] eat the leftover food around the crocodile's teeth. The bird always has something to eat, and the crocodile has clean teeth."
The jacana have big feet.	"Wow! What big feet! Jacanas have feet that are just right for standing on lily pads."

Beginning: **A Fascinating Fact**

Students draw a detailed picture about an animal, person, place, or thing they know about, choose an interesting fact to write about, label it on the picture, and write an engaging sentence that highlights this fact.

Developing: **Fans of Fascinating Facts**

Students brainstorm two facts they know about a topic and then make the facts come alive by writing a interesting sentence for each one.

Extending: **The Amazing Truth**

Students brainstorm one fact they know about a topic and then research to find two additional facts. They make their facts come alive by writing interesting sentences about these facts.

Great Books for This Activity

Picture Books

Pallotta, J. (1989). *The bird alphabet book.* Watertown, MA: Charlesbridge.

Pallotta, J. (1994). *The desert alphabet book.* Watertown, MA: Charlesbridge. (This book contains information about life in deserts around the world.)

St. George, J. (2000). *So you want to be president?* New York: Philomel. (The author of this humorous book reveals unique trivia about presidents of the United States.)

Chapter Book

Berger, M. (1995). *A whale is not a fish and other animal mix-ups.* New York: Scholastic. (This book compares and contrasts animals that people often confuse, such as monkeys and apes or alligators and crocodiles.)

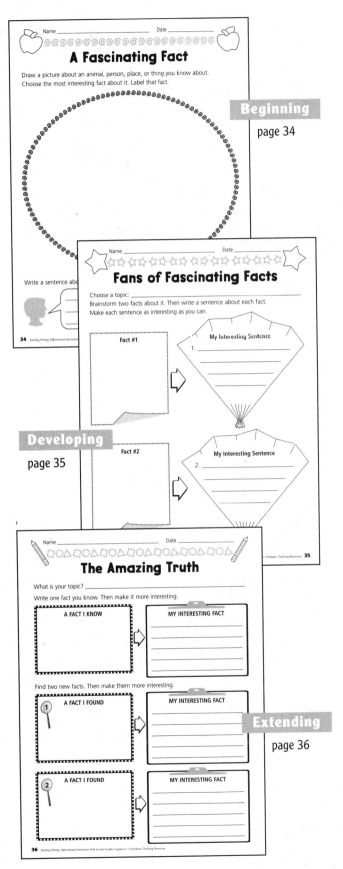

Beginning page 34

Developing page 35

Extending page 36

A Fascinating Fact

Draw a picture about an animal, person, place, or thing you know about. Choose the most interesting fact about it. Label that fact.

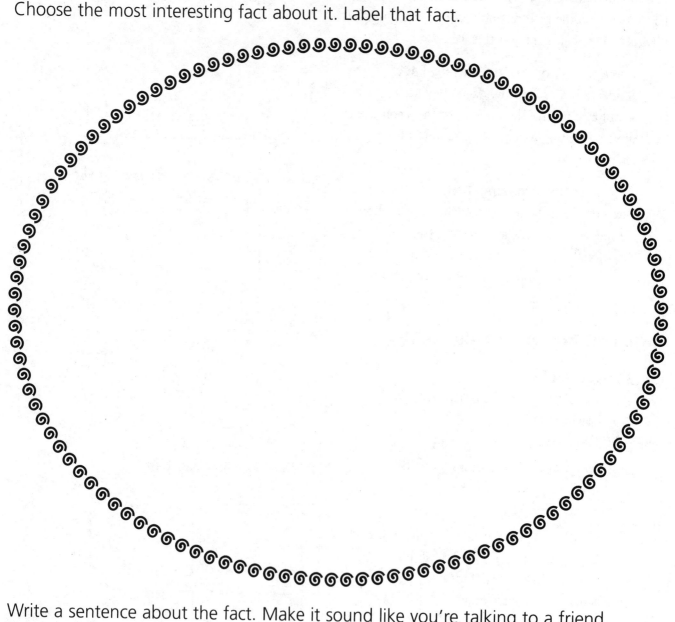

Write a sentence about the fact. Make it sound like you're talking to a friend.

Name _____ Date _____

Fans of Fascinating Facts

Choose a topic: _____.
Brainstorm two facts about it. Then write a sentence about each fact.
Make each sentence as interesting as you can.

Fact #1

My Interesting Sentence

1. _____

_____

_____

_____

Fact #2

My Interesting Sentence

2. _____

_____

_____

_____

Name _____ Date _____

The Amazing Truth

What is your topic? _____

Write one fact you know. Then make it more interesting.

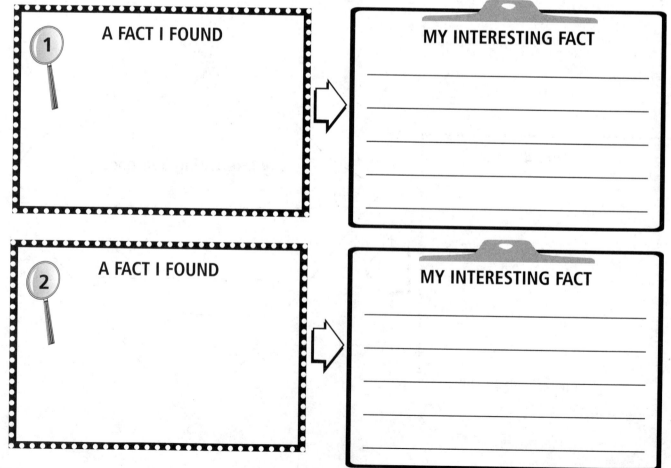

A FACT I KNOW

MY INTERESTING FACT

Find two new facts. Then make them more interesting.

1 **A FACT I FOUND**

MY INTERESTING FACT

2 **A FACT I FOUND**

MY INTERESTING FACT

Creating an Autobiographical Sketch

Skill: *Write a short, factual description of oneself.*

Description

Most children love to publish books they've written. The autobiographical sketch, in which students include important information about themselves, is often an important page in their books, and usually one that they love to write. The autobiographical sketch can be a worthwhile genre study for primary grade students for two reasons: The sketches enable primary grade children to write a short, informational text about a subject they know well—themselves! And, since students may have little or no experience writing in the third person, the sketches provide opportunities for them to write from this perspective. Autobiographical sketches, like personal narratives, bring to life information about authors. There is a major difference between these two genres, however: Personal narratives are often written as stories in which the author describes an event from his or her life, while autobiographical sketches are often written as informational texts that contain facts about the author.

Getting to Know the Concept

You might introduce the idea of an autobiographical sketch by having students reveal something about themselves. For a class of twenty students, you'll need five pieces of different-colored paper with each one cut into four squares. Hand out one square to each student and assign a different question to each color. For example, red: "What do you like to do after school and on the weekends?"; blue: "Do you have any pets? If so, what kind? If not, would you like a pet?"; yellow: "What's your favorite food?"; orange: "What color are your eyes?"; green: "What books or stories have you read or written?"

All students with red squares gather in one part of the room to share information within their small group; students with blue squares are assigned another section of the room as a meeting spot; students with orange squares are assigned a third section, and so forth. After students share information within their groups, they report out to the entire class. This activity offers students an opportunity to share information about themselves.

Teaching the Concept With Literature

You and your students might enjoy collecting examples of autobiographical sketches from the jackets of books you read. There are also many excellent examples of autobiographical sketches online (see, for example, http://www.kidsreads.com/authors/authors.asp, where we suggest you look at the sketches of Cynthia Rylant, Jon Scieszka, and Patricia Polacco). Some sketches are written in first person, some in third person. Reading different sketches will enable you to investigate the type of information included and structure of each one.

Model Lesson

Begin by handing out several different autobiographical sketches that you've collected from book jackets and Web sites. Have children take turns reading them aloud and then talk about the types of information each one contains. List the information on chart paper. Cynthia Rylant, for example, tells where she grew up and what she liked to do as a young child and likes to do as an adult. She lets us know that she lives with her son, Nate, in Oregon. Finally, she explains why she loves being a writer. Also note how Ms. Rylant elaborates on most of her ideas. She doesn't just say she has two dogs and two cats, for instance; she lets us know their names, what they eat, and what they like to do. This interesting additional information shows us more about her as a real person.

Second, look at Jon Scieszka's autobiographical sketch and add to your chart new ideas he includes in his sketch. Explain that Cynthia Rylant's and Jon Scieszka's sketches are written in first person—the authors use the word *I* when talking about themselves.

Third, display Margery Cuyler's autobiographical sketch—which can be found on the back jacket of *Skeleton Hiccups* (2002),

so everyone can see it. After reading it aloud for the children, ask what they notice about this sketch. Children might respond that the sketch is shorter than the others and written in third person (The author uses her name and *she* and *her* instead of *I*). In the sketch, Margery Cuyler also includes interesting information about her house, which she says is supposedly haunted by a ghost. Add these details to the chart paper.

Fourth, review the information you have on the chart paper and ask students what other types of information they might include in their autobiographical sketches. They might mention where they've traveled, their favorite subject in school, and awards/trophies/ribbons they've won. List their responses on the chart paper, and explain that you'll leave the chart posted so they can refer to it if they need help when working on the graphic organizers.

Finally, using the Get to Know Me! or Details About Me graphic organizer, model how to jot down notes about yourself and elaborate on them. Use the notes to demonstrate how to write an autobiographical sketch. Remind children that the sketches will be just a few sentences long, so they need to include and elaborate upon only the information that lets their readers know important and interesting facts about who they are.

Graphic Organizers

When students are familiar with the structure and type of information included in an autobiographical sketch, they are ready for one of the following graphic organizers.

Beginning: **Get to Know Me!**

Students draw a picture or write responses to prompts about their lives. Finally, they use the information on the organizer to write two all-about-me sentences.

Developing: **Details About Me**

Students fill in the chart, listing topics about their lives in the first column and adding details in the second column. They then use three of these ideas to write a few sentences for an autobiographical sketch.

Extending: **Introducing . . . Me!**

Students select four topics that interest them (they may add topics of their own), expand the topics with details, and then write an autobiographical paragraph on the back of the page. (At this level, you may want to give students the option of writing their sketch in first person or third person.)

Great Books for This Activity

Picture Books

See the autobiographical sketches on the jackets of the following books:

Cuyler, M. (2002). *Skeleton hiccups*. New York: Simon & Schuster.

Morales, Y. (2007). *Little night*. New Milford, CT: Roaring Brook Press.

Samuels, B. (2007). *Dolores meets her match*. New York: Farrar, Straus and Giroux.

Chapter Book

Krensky, S. (2001). *Arthur and the goalie ghost*. New York: Little, Brown and Company. (See Brown's autobiographical sketch.)

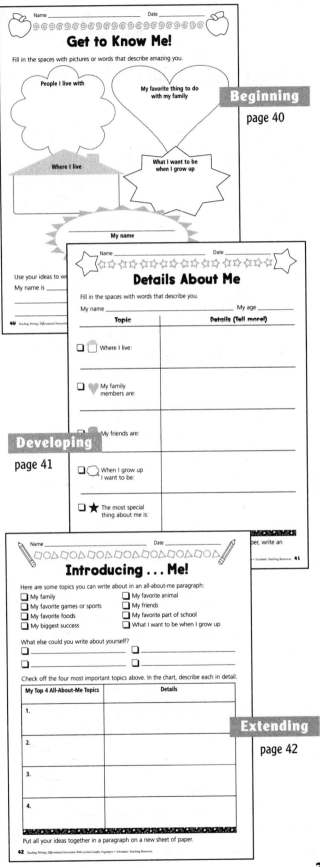

Beginning
page 40

Developing
page 41

Extending
page 42

Name _____ Date _____

Get to Know Me!

Fill in the spaces with pictures or words that describe amazing you.

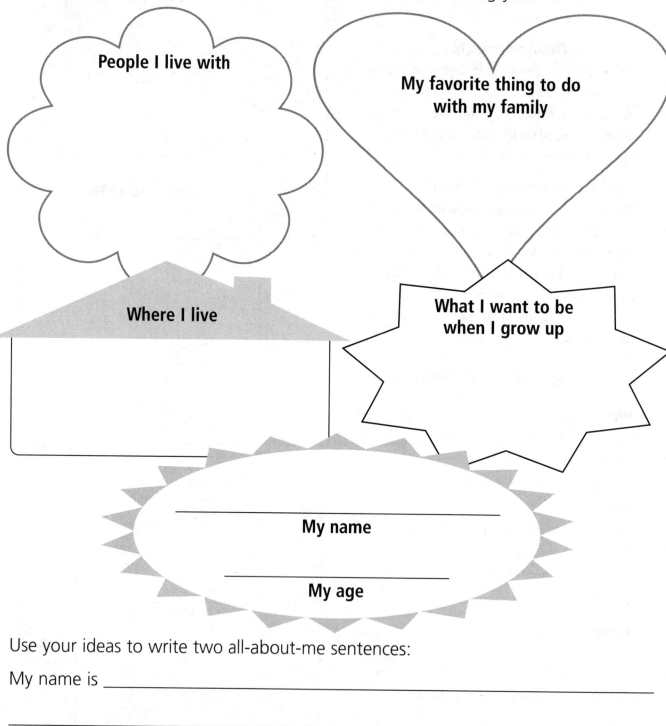

People I live with

My favorite thing to do with my family

Where I live

What I want to be when I grow up

_____
My name

_____
My age

Use your ideas to write two all-about-me sentences:

My name is _____

_____

_____

Details About Me

Fill in the spaces with words that describe you.

My name _____   My age _____

Topic	Details (Tell more!)
❑ 🏠 Where I live:	
❑ 💜 My family members are:	
❑ 👤 My friends are:	
❑ 💭 When I grow up I want to be:	
❑ ★ The most special thing about me is:	

Check three of your ideas from above. Then on a new sheet of paper, write an all-about-me paragraph using those ideas.

Introducing . . . Me!

Here are some topics you can write about in an all-about-me paragraph:

☐ My family   ☐ My favorite animal

☐ My favorite games or sports   ☐ My friends

☐ My favorite foods   ☐ My favorite part of school

☐ My biggest success   ☐ What I want to be when I grow up

What else could you write about yourself?

☐ _____   ☐ _____

☐ _____   ☐ _____

Check off the four most important topics above. In the chart, describe each in detail.

My Top 4 All-About-Me Topics	Details
1.	
2.	
3.	
4.	

Put all your ideas together in a paragraph on a new sheet of paper.

Crafting All-About Books

Skill: *Provide information on one focused topic.*

Note: We recommend teaching this concept after the chapter on Writing Facts That Fascinate.

Description

All-about books provide primary students with a manageable and enjoyable format for learning to read and write nonfiction. These books focus on one topic in which every page (or two-page spread) contains an illustration and one or more factual sentences about a topic. For emergent readers, these books contain limited text that may focus on an animal, a sense, the water cycle, or a profession (e.g., bus driver). You might have examples of all-about books in your classroom library, guided reading collections, or book closet. As young children explore all-about books, they discover that informational writing differs from narrative writing in both content and format.

Getting to Know the Concept

We suggest you read aloud several books that serve as examples of all-about books. When you read, ask children to recall something they notice about the books. They should notice that each book centers around one topic. They might also report the following:

- The books provide factual information about the topic.
- Each page (or every other page) contains a picture or illustration.
- Each page (or every other page) has a sentence (or two).
- The sentences tell about the illustrations.
- The authors use words that we don't usually use (e.g., *joey*).
- Some books contain a table of contents.
- Some contain important words (glossary) at the back of the book.
- Some have a Meet the Author section.

Through these informal read-alouds, you are building awareness of the features that can be present in this important genre for primary grade students.

Teaching the Concept With Literature

Several publishers offer series of books that can serve as models for all-about books. An all-about book at the emergent reading level gives short, concise factual statements about a topic (see, for example, the Learning Center Emergent Readers or Jim Aronosky's All About series, both published by Scholastic). You may find texts that provide interesting variations of this format. For example, some books use rebuses to make the text easier to read (e.g., *Firefighter* by Dana Meachen Rau) or speech bubbles (e.g., *The Case of the Missing Caterpillar: A First Look at the Life Cycle of a Butterfly* and *The Drop Goes Plop: A First Look at the Water Cycle*, both by Sam Godwin).

Model Lesson

This lesson will take more than one day.

Part I: In preparation for this lesson, make a blank big book by stapling together five large pieces of white butcher paper. The top page will be the cover.

Part II: After reading aloud *Koalas* by Gail Saunders-Smith (1998) or another easy informational book, explain that you and your students are going to make an all-about book. Explain that the class all-about book will be an informational book that will follow the same format as *Koalas*.

Return to *Koalas* and point out that the author talks about one important idea on each page (e.g., "A koala climbs trees"). Point out, too, that the sentence on each page tells about the illustration. When students understand these two features of all-about books, determine a topic for the class all-about book, perhaps a topic students have just studied in science or social studies.

With students' help, brainstorm facts about the chosen topic and write them in a list down the left side of the board. After reading aloud the list of facts, discuss which six facts would be most important to include in the class book. Put a checkmark to the right of those six facts. Next, discuss the order in which the six facts should appear in the class book and number each fact to indicate the sequence. If the facts are not already written in complete, interesting sentences with

content vocabulary (e.g., *joey*), talk about how you can revise them.

Part III: Type the six sentences using a large point size, print the text, and glue one sentence on the front and back of the second, third, and fourth pages. Either illustrate each page with students' help or have the children illustrate the pages.

Part IV: Return to *Koalas* and point out the table of contents (page 3). Discuss the purpose of a table of contents and demonstrate how to create one for your all-about book. Write the table of contents on the back of the first page. Talk about why you waited until you completed your book to create the table of contents. Students using the Developing and Extended graphic organizers will include this feature.

Part V: Show the Words to Know page (glossary, page 22) in *Koalas*, and discuss the purpose of this text feature. On the last page of your class book, write "Words to Know" and have students help you select three words that might be important and unfamiliar to readers of your book (e.g., *bud, roots, stem*). Using a think-aloud, write the words under "Words to Know" and, with input from students, write the definitions. This activity prepares students for the Extended graphic organizer.

Graphic Organizers

When students understand that all-about books contain relevant facts about one topic, they are ready to complete one of the graphic organizers. They may write books about an animal (e.g., a pet or an endangered animal), a place (e.g., a dentist's office), an occupation (e.g., a firefighter), or a topic from your science or social studies curriculum.

Beginning: **An All-About Book You Can't Live Without**

Students select a topic. They draw pictures to depict three facts about their topic. Finally, they write a factual sentence to go with each illustration.

Developing: **An All-About Book Worth Shouting About**

Students supply an all-about book title. They write the factual information they want to include on pages 1, 2, 3, and 4 of their books. Last, they complete a table of contents.

Extending: **An Out-Of-This-World All-About Book**

Students design all-about books as described in the Developing graphic organizer. On a new sheet of paper, they add a glossary, listing three or four important words and defining them.

Great Books for This Activity

Picture Books

Godwin, S. (1999). *The case of the missing caterpillar: A first look at the life cycle of a butterfly.* Minneapolis, MN: Picture Window Books.

Godwin, S. (1998). *The drop goes plop: A first look at the water cycle.* Minneapolis, MN: Picture Window Books.

Rau, D. M. (2008). *Firefighter.* New York: Marshall Cavendish Benchmark.

Saunders-Smith, G. (1998). *Koalas.* Mankato, MN: Pebble Books.

Vern, A. (2000). *Where do frogs come from?* New York: Harcourt. (This book simply describes the transformation from egg, to tadpole, to frog.)

Chapter Book

Micucci, C. (2003). *The life and times of the ant.* Boston: Houghton Mifflin. (This chaptered picture book describes all aspects of ant characteristics.)

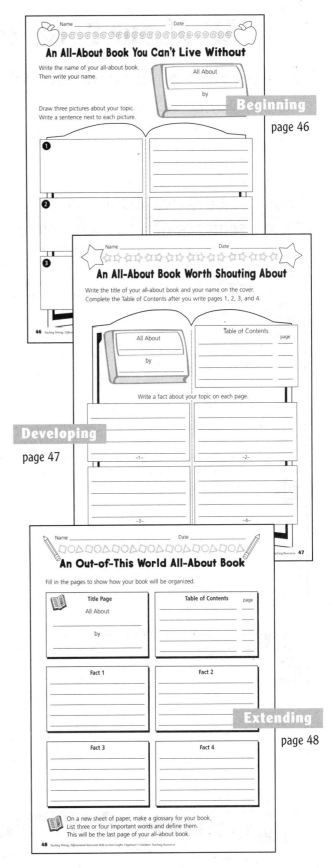

page 46

page 47

page 48

An All-About Book You Can't Live Without

Write the name of your all-about book.
Then write your name.

All About
_____

by

_____

Draw three pictures about your topic.
Write a sentence next to each picture.

①

_____
_____
_____
_____

②

_____
_____
_____
_____

③

_____
_____
_____
_____
_____

An All-About Book Worth Shouting About

Write the title of your all-about book and your name on the cover.
Complete the Table of Contents after you write pages 1, 2, 3, and 4.

All About
_____
by
_____

Table of Contents   page
_____ _____
_____ _____
_____ _____
_____ _____

Write a fact about your topic on each page.

–1–

–2–

–3–

–4–

An Out-of-This World All-About Book

Fill in the pages to show how your book will be organized.

Title Page	Table of Contents

Title Page

All About

_____

by

_____

Table of Contents   page

_____ _____

_____ _____

_____ _____

_____ _____

Fact 1

_____

_____

_____

_____

Fact 2

_____

_____

_____

_____

Fact 3

_____

_____

_____

_____

Fact 4

_____

_____

_____

_____

 On a new sheet of paper, make a glossary for your book.
List three or four important words and define them.
This will be the last page of your all-about book.

Exploring How-To Writing

Skill: *Write instructions on how to do or make something.*

Description

How-to writing (also known as informative narrative or procedural writing) instructs a reader how to make or do something. Safety tips, recipes, game directions, and art projects are how-to texts that children frequently read. The how-to text is sequential and is written in the imperative as a command. The writing must be clear and include time-order signal words, such as *first, then, next,* and *last,* or number words. We recommend that students visualize the process when writing. "Viewing" each step of the process aids them in including all the necessary steps.

Getting to Know the Concept

Begin by explaining that how-to writing gives step-by-step directions on how to do or make something. Use very simple directions to model the task of how to erase the board. Show students each step in the process, and then write the steps on the board. The steps might look like this:

- First, pick up the eraser.
- Next, place the eraser close to the writing you want to erase.
- Last, rub the eraser back and forth on the board.

Next, to help young children understand the how-to concept, get their bodies moving. Tell them that you are going to give them step-by-step directions to follow. Explain that they must listen to each "command" to complete the directions correctly. Write the directions in the first column of a chart (see below), but don't reveal the action. Let students identify each action. Then write their responses in the second column. If you label the action—such as waving hello or good-bye— prior to giving the directions, students may miss the importance of giving clear, step-by-step instructions. Other actions you might try include lining up, opening the door, and doing a jumping jack.

Step-by-Step Directions	Action Name
First, bend your arm upward at the elbow. Next, open your hand wide and move it side to side three times. Last, put your arm down by your side.	Waving hello or good-bye

Teaching the Concept With Literature

There are many how-to books written for children. Those that explain how to make crafts, how to do science experiments, or how to follow simple recipes often provide good models. *All in Just One Cookie* (Goodman, 2006) is a delightful and unusual procedural text that has a story line, along with a chocolate chip cookie recipe. As Grandma makes cookies, the dog and cat explore the origin of each of the ingredients. The recipe on the last page gives an excellent example of how-to writing.

When you read aloud this text to students, explain that the author shows what Grandma is doing: "Grandma adds and blends, making sure each speck of white disappears into the mix." In the how-to recipe, the author tells the reader what to do: "Combine the butter, white sugar, brown sugar and vanilla extract in a large bowl." *All in Just One Cookie* helps students understand that how-to texts use commands to tell the reader exactly what to do.

Model Lesson

Begin the lesson on how-to writing by explaining the criteria for giving clear directions:
- Write the directions step by step.
- Write the steps in order.
- Use command verbs, such as *stir*, *jump*, or *turn*.
- Use signal words to help the reader understand the sequence, such as *first*, *next*, *then*, and *last*.

Have students visualize how to make a call to 9-1-1 to help someone and then ask what they "see." Write the steps they volunteer in sequential order on the board. If necessary, remind students to use command words to give directions. Their how-to might look like this:

Steps to Make an Emergency Call
1. Pick up the phone.
2. Listen for the dial tone.
3. Press the numbers 9-1-1 in order.
4. Tell what the emergency is.
5. Tell your name and address.
6. Answer any questions the 911 operator asks.
7. Try to stay calm.

Talk about the signal words (*first*, *next*, *then*, and *last*) and how we can use them to turn the above list of steps into a paragraph. Work together to write the paragraph, pointing out where the signal words should be placed. Remind students that the first line of the paragraph should be indented. Show that a comma goes after each signal word. Once the paragraph is written, discuss whether a reader could follow the directions. Your model paragraph may look like this:

First, pick up the phone. Next, listen for the dial tone. Then, push the numbers on the buttons in order: 9, 1, 1. When the operator answers, tell what the emergency is and give your name and address. Finally, answer any questions the operator asks. Try to stay calm.

Repeat this procedure with other how-to activities—for example, stapling papers, sharpening a pencil, getting a glass of water, or preparing a bowl of cereal. First, have students visualize the steps in each task. Next, write the directions in a chart. Then, write the paragraphs and include signal words. Next, talk about using the words *next* or *then* more than once if necessary. Finally, visualize the steps again to see if the reader can do the activity following the directions.

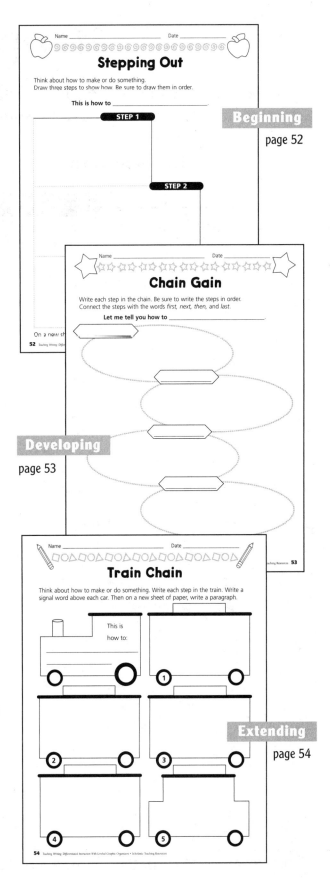

Graphic Organizers

When students can accurately give each other directions to do something, they are ready for one of the graphic organizers. Here are some suggestions for how-to writing prompts: crossing the street safely, reporting a fire, making a peanut butter sandwich, preparing popcorn in the microwave, brushing your teeth, or putting on a coat.

Beginning: **Stepping Out**

Students draw three steps to show how to do or make something. They write directions based on their illustrations.

Developing: **Chain Gain**

Students write four steps to show how to do or make something. They use signal words to show the order of the steps, and then write a paragraph.

Extending: **Train Chain**

Students write five steps to give directions to do or make something. They write a paragraph with the directions and include appropriate signal words.

Great Books for This Activity

Picture Books

Fisher, C. (2008) *The snow show*. Orlando: Harcourt. (In addition to sharing scientific information, this book shows how snow is made. For instance, Fisher writes, "First, warm some water with sunshine." Then she goes on to discuss evaporation.)

Goodman, S. E. (2006) *All in just one cookie*. New York: Greenwillow Books. (This book contains sections on each cookie ingredient, and the text structure is a bit more complex than a simple picture book.)

Chapter Book

Pfiffner, G. (1996) *Earth-friendly outdoor fun: How to make fabulous games, gardens, and other projects from reusable objects*. New York: Wiley and Sons.

Beginning
page 52

Developing
page 53

Extending
page 54

Stepping Out

Think about how to make or do something.
Draw three steps to show how. Be sure to draw them in order.

This is how to _____.

STEP 1

STEP 2

STEP 3

On a new sheet of paper, write each step. Be sure they are in order.

Chain Gain

Write each step in the chain. Be sure to write the steps in order.
Connect the steps with the words *first, next, then,* and *last.*

Let me tell you how to _____.

_____

_____

_____

_____

On a new sheet of paper, write your how-to paragraph.
Connect the steps with the words *first, next, then,* and *last.*

Train Chain

Think about how to make or do something. Write each step in the train. Write a signal word above each car. Then on a new sheet of paper, write a paragraph.

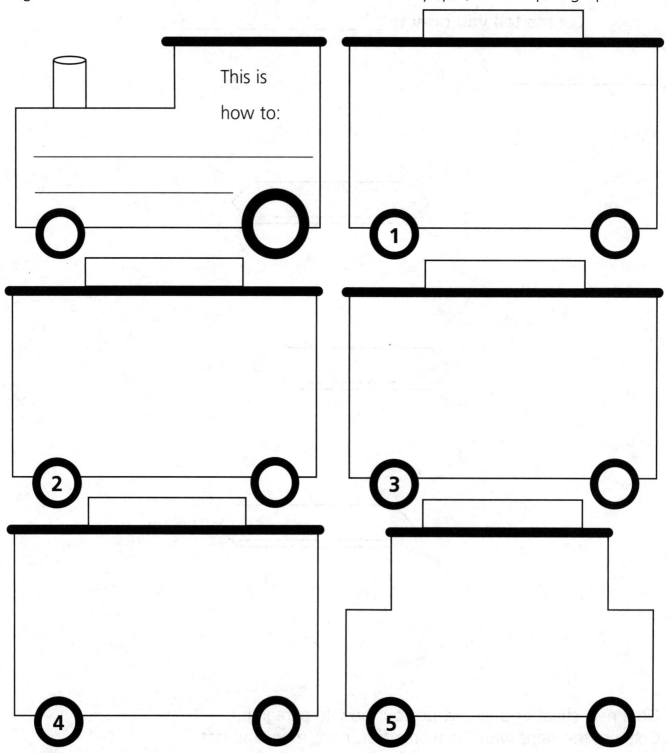

This is
how to:
_____
_____

1

2

3

4

5

Exploring Persuasive Writing

Skill: *Convince others to agree with your idea.*

Description

Most of us have overheard recess conversations in which one student successfully convinces a classmate to trade snacks, or we have had a student assert why he or she should be the one to take the class pet home for spring vacation. Students often present compelling oral arguments. Yet, when asked to write persuasively, whether for authentic purposes—such as "applying" for a classroom job (e.g., the person who waters the plants)—or for high-stakes tests, many writers struggle.

Our ultimate goal when teaching persuasive writing is to have students take a stand, think of logical reasons to support it, supply examples to shore up those reasons, and bring closure to the paragraph that reminds readers of their stand.

Getting to Know the Concept

Ask questions such as the following to initiate a discussion: "Do you think Amelia Bedelia (or another character from literature) would make a good friend? Why? Why not?"

After students share answers, informally talk about the elements of persuasion:

- A stand—what the writer wants the reader to know, think, or do ("I want everyone to know that Amelia Bedelia would be a great friend.")
- Reasons that support the stand ("Amelia Bedelia is funny.")
- Details that can be used to elaborate on the reasons ("When Amelia Bedelia is told to dust the furniture, she adds dust instead of taking the dust off.")
- A conclusion or a reminder of the stand ("That's why I think Amelia Bedelia would make a great friend.")

Teaching the Concept With Literature

Finding books that have elements of persuasion in them can be challenging, but *Click, Clack, Moo: Cows That Type* (Cronin, 2000) provides a humorous example. The book begins with a letter the cows type to the farmer. In it, the cows state what they want (electric blankets) and tell why this is a good idea (the barn is cold). As you read the book aloud to your students, point out what each animal

wants the farmer to do, why the animals want the farmer to do these things, and whether or not the animals are persuasive.

Model Lesson

For this lesson, we suggest using *I Wanna Iguana* (Orloff, 2004). In this story, Alex tries to convince his mother to let him adopt an iguana. Start by reading aloud the first letter Alex writes to his mother, discuss what Alex wants, and write it in the first column of a chart like the one shown below. In the second column, list reasons Alex gives to support his request for the iguana. In the third column, list details he uses to elaborate on his reasons. Finally, show students how to bring closure to a persuasive piece. A conclusion strategy might be as simple as restating what the author wants: "That's why I think I should be able to adopt Mikey's iguana." Your completed chart might look like the one below.

Next, have children help you fill in the first three columns of a similar chart about something they might want to convince their parents about, such as "to stay up late to watch a movie" (first column). Keeping their audience in mind, students supply reasons to support their stand (second column). They might say, "My friends are going to stay up to watch the movie." "I can sleep late tomorrow." "I've never seen this movie." Record each reason on the chart. Then have students elaborate on each reason and record their responses (third column): "I'm a year older than Sharon and she can stay up." Work with students on how to state their conclusion persuasively.

Conclude by pointing out that every persuasive piece should contain all three parts–a beginning (the stand or statement of what the author wants), a middle (reasons and details), and an end (the conclusion) and that each part serves a unique purpose.

Graphic Organizers

When students can verbalize what they want, identify at least one reason to support their idea, and provide a closing, they are ready for one of the graphic organizers. Students might try to convince you to give less homework, cafeteria workers to offer more lunch choices, or their parents to take them to a baseball game or to buy a favorite toy.

What I Want	Here's Why My Idea Is a Good One	In Fact …	Conclusion
to adopt Mikey Gulligan's baby iguana when he moves	If I take the iguana, Mikey's dog won't eat it.		
	Iguanas are quiet and cute.	Iguanas are cuter than hamsters.	
	He's small and you won't have to see him.	I can keep him in a cage in my room.	
			That's why I think I should be able to adopt Mikey's iguana.

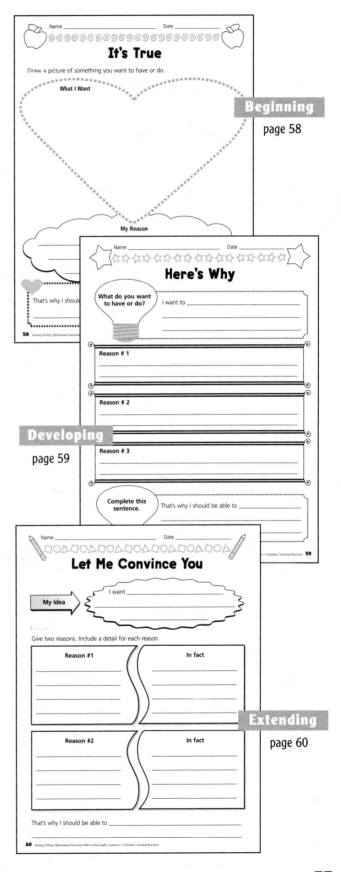

Beginning: **It's True**

Students draw a picture to show something they want, give a reason, and complete the sentence "That's why I should be able to . . ."

Developing: **Here's Why**

Students identify something they want, supply three reasons for their stand, and complete the sentence "That's why I should be able to . . ."

Extending: **Let Me Convince You**

Students identify something they want and supply two reasons for their idea. Then they include one detail for each reason, and complete the sentence "That's why I should be able to . . ."

Great Books for This Activity

Picture Books

Cronin, D. (2000). *Click, clack, moo: Cows that type.* New York: Simon & Schuster.

Orlof, K. K. (2004). *I wanna iguana.* New York: G. P. Putnam's Sons.

Palatini, M. (2003). *The perfect pet.* New York: HarperCollins. (A girl tries to convince her parents to get her a dog, cat, or horse and has a rationale for each one.)

Willems, M. (2006). *Don't let the pigeon stay up late!* New York: Hyperion. (A pigeon tries to convince the reader that he should be able to stay up late.)

Chapter Book

McDonald, M. (2005). *Judy Moody declares independence.* Cambridge, MA: Candlewick. (Judy tries to convince her family that she should receive a higher allowance, her own bathroom, and other freedoms.)

Name _____ Date ___

It's True

Draw a picture of something you want to have or do.

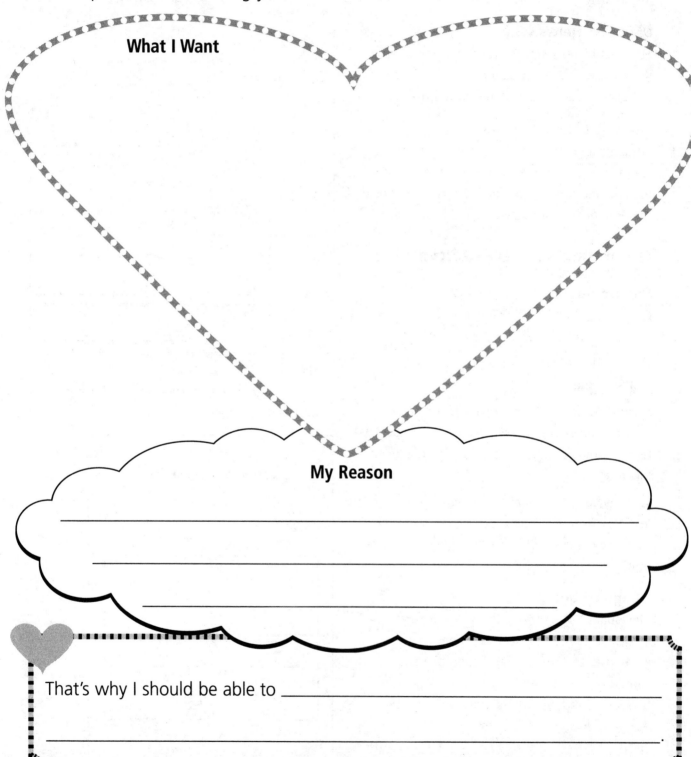

What I Want

My Reason

_____

_____

_____

That's why I should be able to _____

_____.

Name _____ Date _____

Here's Why

What do you want to have or do?

I want to _____

_____

_____.

Reason # 1

_____

_____

Reason # 2

_____

_____

Reason # 3

_____

_____

Complete this sentence.

That's why I should be able to _____

_____

_____.

Let Me Convince You

My Idea ➡

I want _____

_____

_____ .

Give two reasons. Include a detail for each reason.

Reason #1	In fact
_____	_____
_____	_____
_____	_____
_____	_____

Reason #2	In fact
_____	_____
_____	_____
_____	_____
_____	_____

That's why I should be able to _____

_____ .

Describing a Character: Outside

Skill: *Describe the physical traits of a character.*

Description

Characters can be portrayed in different ways, but we mainly think of character descriptions as including physical appearance and personality. To teach primary students how to write a character description, begin by having them describe what the character looks like. The concreteness of a character's physical appearance is less complex than the personality traits, so it's an easier entry for teaching character description. Students describe facial features, body features, clothing and all items that are part of the character's outward appearance giving as many sensory details as possible.

Getting to Know the Concept

Place a girl or boy character on a felt board and change the character's clothes and accessories. (You can also use paper dolls.) Begin by describing the facial features of the character. For example, the boy has brown eyes, dark hair, and a turned-up nose. Then offer words to describe the outfit. You might say the boy is wearing new blue jeans with a black belt and an orange T-shirt. After changing the outfit, give a description of the new outfit, such as brown pants with a blue and brown striped shirt. Change the character's outfit a few more times and have students describe the clothes. Elaborate for them when necessary. Explain that you are describing what a person looks like. This is called a character description or the "outside" description of a character.

Teaching the Concept With Literature

Literature offers multiple opportunities to share wonderful models of character descriptions with students. In *My Great-Aunt Arizona*, Gloria Houston (1992) writes, "Arizona was a very tall little girl. She wore her long brown hair in braids. She wore long full dresses, and a pretty white apron. She wore high-button shoes, and many petticoats, too."

When students read, have them visualize what the author is saying so they can "see" what is being described. In the case of Arizona, students will easily connect with and visualize "tall" and "brown hair in braids." Talk about the descriptions and which words help us "see" the character.

Model Lesson

Explain that writers give details so readers will have a clear picture of a character's appearance. Invite students to look at a picture of a person and offer words that describe him or her. Create a list of those details. For example, to describe a photo of a tennis player, students may come up with responses like those in List 1 below.

When this list of words is complete, tell students that when they write character descriptions they should use describing words to give lots of details. Work with them to generate details and more descriptive information about the person in the picture. Record their ideas in a second list. To emphasize the contrast, place the lists side by side like the one below.

Use students' descriptive words in List 2 to begin the first sentences of a character description. Then ask volunteers to help you continue to write a paragraph describing the "outside" of this character. Your class paragraph might look something like the following:

The tennis player is an old man. He is dressed in a red collared shirt with buttons near the top and red shorts that have a white stripe down each side. He is also wearing long white socks with red stripes near the top and white tennis shoes with a red stripe on the side. On his head, the man wears rimless sunglasses. A white headband is tucked behind his ears. On the player's left wrist is a white wristband, and he's gripping a wooden tennis racket.

Ask students what they can tell about the character from the written description. This lesson can be repeated with a different picture or item—a superhero figure, nesting doll, or stuffed animal in your classroom. Students need to be comfortable giving details and descriptive words before writing a character description independently.

Graphic Organizers

When students can accurately describe the "outside" attributes of a character and understand how this description provides

List 1	List 2
man	smiling old man
shirt	red shirt with collar and buttons at top
shorts	red shorts with a white stripe down each side
socks	long white socks with red stripe near the top
tennis shoes	white tennis shoes with a red stripe on the side
head band	white headband tucked behind ears
sunglasses	rimless sunglasses
wristband	white wristband on left wrist
hands	hands gripping wooden tennis racket

important information about that character, they are ready to complete one of the following graphic organizers:

Beginning: **Look Who's Here**
Students draw a picture of a character and write two sentences describing him or her.

Developing: **What a Character!**
Students draw a picture of a character, list details about his or her appearance, and write three sentences describing the character.

Extending: **Shopping for a Character**
Students list details about a character's appearance, add more descriptive words to three of these details, and write a three-to-four sentence character description.

Great Books for This Activity

Picture Books

Brown, J. (1964). *Flat Stanley*. New York: Scholastic. (The first chapter describes a very, very flat Stanley.)

Houston, G. (1992). *My great-aunt Arizona*. New York: HarperCollins.

Woodruff, E. (1999). *The memory coat*. New York: Scholastic. (In this touching book, a young boy is reluctant to give up a coat that he has outgrown because it was made by his deceased mother.)

Chapter Book

Dahl, R. (1995). *The magic finger*. New York: Puffin Books. (Pages 12 and 13 describe the teacher growing whiskers and a tail.)

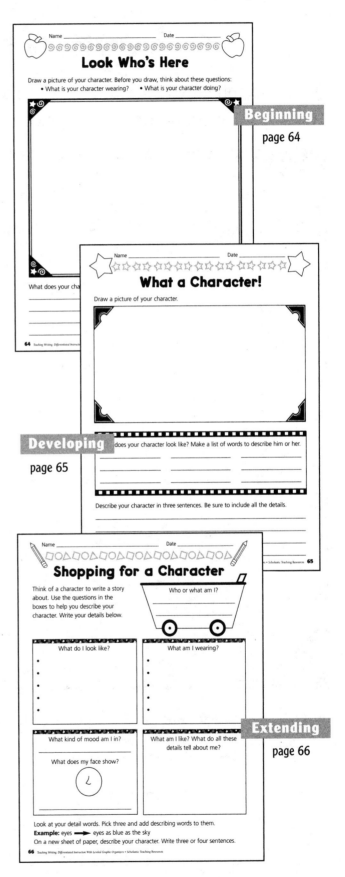

Look Who's Here — **Beginning** page 64

What a Character! — **Developing** page 65

Shopping for a Character — **Extending** page 66

Name _____ Date _____

Look Who's Here

Draw a picture of your character. Before you draw, think about these questions:
- What is your character wearing?
- What is your character doing?

What does your character look like? Write two sentences to describe him or her.

_____

_____

_____

_____

What a Character!

Draw a picture of your character.

What does your character look like? Make a list of words to describe him or her.

_____ _____ _____

_____ _____ _____

_____ _____ _____

Describe your character in three sentences. Be sure to include all the details.

_____

_____

_____

_____

Name _____   Date _____

Shopping for a Character

Think of a character to write a story about. Use the questions in the boxes to help you describe your character. Write your details below.

Who or what am I?

_____

_____

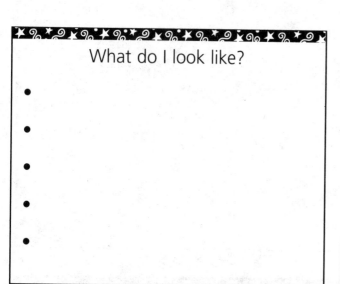

What do I look like?

-
-
-
-
-

What am I wearing?

-
-
-
-
-

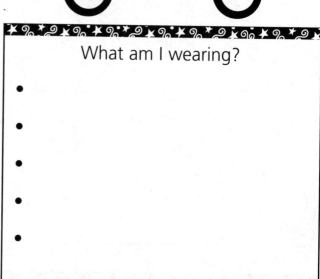

What kind of mood am I in?

_____

What does my face show?

What am I like? What do all these details tell about me?

Look at your detail words. Pick three and add describing words to them.

Example: eyes ➡ eyes as blue as the sky

On a new sheet of paper, describe your character. Write three or four sentences.

Describing a Character: Inside

Skill: *Describe the personality of a character.*

Description

Characters are described by their appearance (the "outside") and their personality (the "inside"). A character's personality can be described not only through adjectives and other descriptive words, but it also can be implied by his or her actions. Character descriptions should give a clear picture of the character and suggest how that character might act because of his or her personality traits. Understanding a character's personality allows students to make accurate inferences and predictions and draw logical conclusions.

Getting to Know the Concept

Begin teaching the notion of personality by leading a discussion on how some people or animals can be mean, nice, angry, kind, or crabby. Explain that these words describe the personality or "inside" of a person or character.

Ask students to watch and listen carefully as you act out a personality, so they can describe your "inside" characteristics. For example, you might play "Sam" and walk in front of the class with a noticeable frown and glaring eyes, saying "I have had a miserable day! The waitress was so mixed up she forgot to give me a second cup of coffee, and I called her over twice to remind her. I didn't leave a tip. Then I had to scoot my neighbor's dog out of my yard. He always makes a mess. That's why I don't like dogs. I even had to yell at the newspaper boy for bringing my paper late."

After the role-play, complete a three-column chart like the one shown below that reveals Sam's personality. Ask students what words they would use to describe Sam and write their responses in the first column under List 1. Then have them add details to each descriptive word and write the more thorough descriptions in the second column under List 2. Finally, ask what Sam did that made students come up with these descriptions and write their responses in the third column under "What Sam Did."

List 1	List 2	What Sam Did
mean	a yelling, mean man	yelled at paperboy
crabby	a very crabby man	crabby to waitress, dog
stingy	a stingy, unfair old man	no tip for waitress
dog-hating	a horrible dog-hating man	said he didn't like dogs

Then ask students to help you write a two-or-three-sentence description stating Sam's inside characteristics, such as the following: *Sam is a mean, crabby person. He is a horrible dog-hating man. He is also stingy and unfair.*

Teaching the Concept With Literature

When you read books to the class, take the opportunity to point out examples of strong character descriptions and discuss the descriptive language found in these works. You might use "Jack Russell and the Beanstalk," an excellent model that can be found in *Dog Tales* (Rae, 1998). The author writes, "Jack had lots of good qualities—he was quick, he could crawl into small spaces, he could even climb trees. But Jack did have a few shortcomings. For one thing, he was determined. Doggedly determined. And he was stubborn. In fact, Jack was downright dogmatic." When reading descriptions like this, point out how the descriptive words help us get to know the character's personality.

Model Lesson

Tell students to close their eyes and think about a character they would like to create for a story. After students have thought about their characters, ask for some words that describe the characters' personalities. On the board or chart paper, write down these words. Your chart might look something like the List 1 column in the chart below. Then challenge students to tell you more about this aspect of their character and write their expanded phrases in the List 2 column. To encourage more in-depth descriptions, you might ask students to think about how other characters who talk to or work with this character might describe him or her. Finally, in the List 3 column, write what the character might do—what action or behavior could occur—because of that characteristic.

Using the chart, model a description of the "inside" of a character with students' help. Your description may look like this: *Jared was a very happy little boy, who laughed all the time. He was so kind and said nice things to his friends. Jared was always generous and would even give his own toys away.*

Keep your word chart available for students' independent writing time. Add descriptive words to the chart whenever possible. Encourage students to find words in their reading that can be added to the chart.

List 1 Word	List 2 More Description	List 3 Action
happy	very happy	laugh
angry	extremely angry	yell
kind	so kind	help someone
stingy	really, really stingy	be cheap with money
generous	always generous	give toys away
cranky	too cranky	act mad
stubborn	dreadfully stubborn	refuse to do something
nervous	terribly nervous	twirl hair around finger

Graphic Organizers

When students can accurately describe a character's "inside" characteristics, they are ready to complete one of the following graphic organizers:

Beginning: **What's Inside?**

Students draw a picture of a character and write two sentences describing his or her personality.

Developing: **Personality Plus**

Students list three words that describe a character's personality and circle "a little" or "very" to show the degree. They provide an action for each word and then write a description using these details.

Extending: **Inside Out**

Students list words that describe a character's personality, then add adjectives or adverbs to enhance them. They list actions that would stem from these character traits. Finally, students write a character description that includes these traits and actions.

Great Books for This Activity

Picture Books

Lundell, M. (1995). *A girl named Helen Keller.* New York: Scholastic. (Chapter 2 has an unusual description of Helen's personality.)

Rae, J. (1998). *Dog tales.* Berkeley, CA: Tricycle Press. (This book contains a number of piggyback fairy tales containing character descriptions.)

Chapter Book

Dahl, R. (1998). *George's marvelous medicine.* New York: Puffin. (This humorous book contains rather unpleasant descriptions of George's grandmother.)

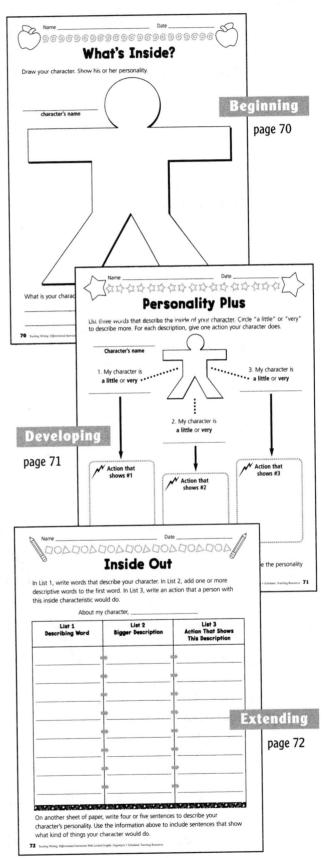

page 70

page 71

page 72

What's Inside?

Draw your character. Show his or her personality.

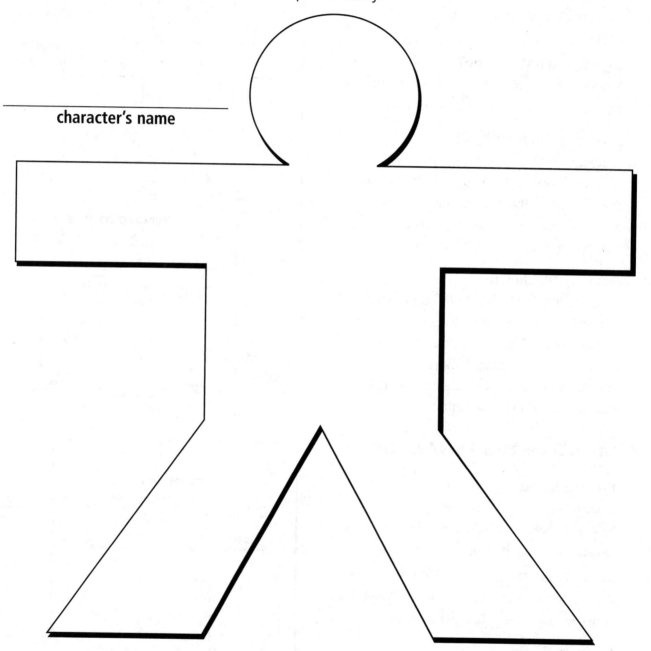

_____
character's name

What is your character like inside? Write two sentences.

_____

_____

Personality Plus

List three words that describe the inside of your character. Circle "a little" or "very" to describe more. For each description, give one action your character does.

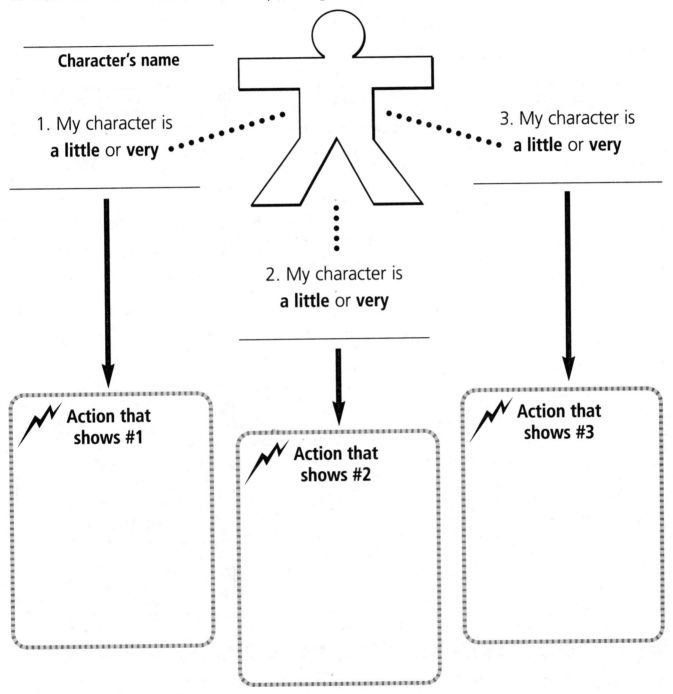

_____
Character's name

1. My character is
a little or **very**

3. My character is
a little or **very**

2. My character is
a little or **very**

⚡ **Action that shows #1**

⚡ **Action that shows #2**

⚡ **Action that shows #3**

On a new sheet of paper, write three or four sentences that describe the personality of your character. Use the details you listed here.

Inside Out

In List 1, write words that describe your character. In List 2, add one or more descriptive words to the first word. In List 3, write an action that a person with this inside characteristic would do.

About my character, _____

| List 1
Describing Word | List 2
Bigger Description | List 3
Action That Shows
This Description |
|---|---|---|
| | | |
| | | |
| | | |
| | | |
| | | |
| | | |
| | | |
| | | |

On another sheet of paper, write four or five sentences to describe your character's personality. Use the information above to include sentences that show what kind of things your character would do.

Understanding Plot

Skill: *Write a simple story plot.*

Description

The plot is usually the crux of a story. Plot includes the problem (or problems) in the story, the attempts to solve it, and the solution. A rise in action within the plot leads to the solution. Often, children write stories with flat story lines, in which there is no rise in action. For instance, a story may be written about a boy walking to the store and walking back home, which does not include a problem. On the other hand, some children introduce so many characters and problems that the story becomes extremely confusing. These are the students who can write a story about a hero in a spaceship fighting five different enemies at the same time; the action becomes so involved that the story ends abruptly or is never finished. To help students write interesting and well-defined stories, it is important they know that stories usually include one or more characters, a setting, a problem, attempts to solve the problem, and a solution.

Getting to Know the Concept

To make the concept of plot real to students, first talk to them about a time you had a problem and how you solved it and then ask them to share their own experiences. You might get scenarios such as running late for school or forgetting lunch. Ask how the problem was solved, and if there were any other ways the problem could have been solved. Using a scenario of missing the school bus, set up a chart like the one shown below. Let students generate different ways the problem could be solved and then offer a solution.

Explain that when we write a story, we use different attempts to solve a problem to make our story more interesting. We probably wouldn't think of taking a helicopter or a horse to school, but these "unusual, but doable" solutions might add interest to a story.

Problem	How problem could be solved	Solution
Missed the school bus	Get a ride from Mom or Dad Get a ride from Grandma or Grandpa Walk Take the city bus Ride your bike Take a helicopter Ride a horse	Got a ride from Mom

Teaching the Concept With Literature

In the case of plot, we suggest that you share two different types of books with your students. *Owl Moon* (Yolen, 1987) is a memoir with a straight story line and no rising action. The author and grandfather visit the woods to see owls at night. When you read this or a similar book to your students, reveal that there is no problem in this story. Then explain that some books are written just to describe events, as in *Owl Moon*. Ask your students how this book differs from the story of "The Three Little Pigs." Emphasize the problem (the wolf destroys houses in an attempt to get the pigs), the attempts to solve it (the pigs go to the next house so they won't get eaten), and the solution (the brick house is strong enough to save the pigs). Explain that you want students to write stories that have a plot, which is the problem, how the character tries to fix the problem, and the solution.

Model Lesson

Begin the lesson on plot by reminding students that the plot of a story includes a problem, attempts to solve it, and a solution. Tell students that as authors they can generate a number of plot ideas. Prepare a chart like the one shown below. Pose a problem such as the following: "Ava's dog, Julius, broke loose from his leash, and now Ava cannot find him." This problem sets up a story with two characters and an outdoor setting.

Use the "think, pair, share" strategy to get students to generate ideas about how this problem could be solved. Write students' suggestions on the chart, making sure there is at least one "unusual, but doable" attempt. The class should then choose two or three solutions that Ava will try in the story. Number these on the chart so students can refer to them when they're writing. Have the class pick a solution and write it on the chart. Your finished chart may look something like the one shown below.

This simple plot has two attempts, and Ava is successful with the second attempt. With students' help, model writing the story.

In a subsequent lesson, use the same chart structure and have students generate story ideas with a main problem, attempts to solve the problem, and a solution. Guide them though class writing as you model how the pieces go together.

Graphic Organizers

When students can generate problems and solutions and offer suggestions for writing the plot, they are ready for one of the graphic

Problem	How problem could be solved	Solution
Ava's dog, Julius, broke loose from his leash, and now Ava cannot find him.	Ava can call for the dog. (1) Ava can look around the neighborhood. Ava can ask her friends for help. Ava can use her bike to find Julius. (2) Ava can put a mirror on a kite and look for the dog through the mirror.	Ava used her bike and found Julius in the neighbor's yard.

organizers. If necessary, you might suggest the following problems: finding a kitten or puppy, missing a shoe, wanting to buy a new toy, or sharing a bedroom.

Beginning: **Plot Plan**

Students draw character(s), a problem, and the solution. They then write a simple story.

Developing: **The Scheme of Things**

Students list a character or characters, generate a problem, offer two attempts to solve it, and choose the best solution. They use these elements to write a story.

Extending: **The Plot Thickens**

Students list characters, generate a problem; offer three or four attempts to solve the problem, including one that's unusual but doable, and a solution. They choose three attempts to include in a story.

Great Books for This Activity

Picture Books

Butler, M. C. (2006). *One winter day.* New York: Scholastic. (This book has a very simple plot that is easy to follow.)

Kraus, R. (1945). *The carrot seed.* New York: Scholastic. (A young child keeps trying to grow a carrot and uses different attempts to solve his problem.)

Yolen, J. (1987). *Owl moon.* New York: Philomel.

Chapter Book

Dahl, R. (1980). *The Twits.* New York: Puffin. (This enjoyable book has a hilarious problem in almost every chapter.)

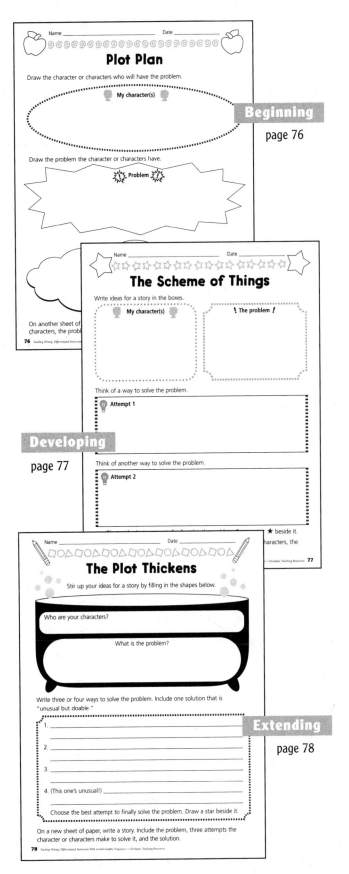

Name _____ Date _____

Plot Plan

Draw the character or characters who will have the problem.

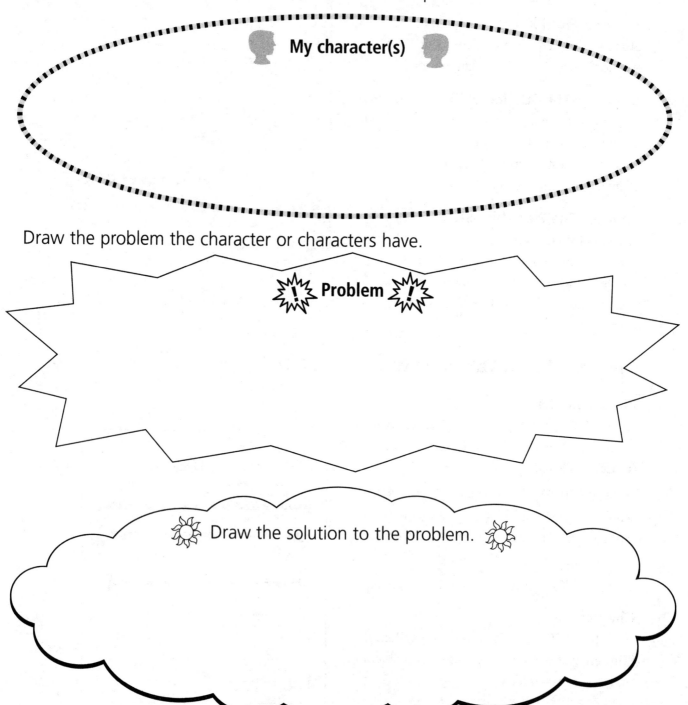

My character(s)

Draw the problem the character or characters have.

Problem

Draw the solution to the problem.

On another sheet of paper, write a story that tells about the character or characters, the problem, and how it was solved.

Name _____ Date _____

The Scheme of Things

Write ideas for a story in the boxes.

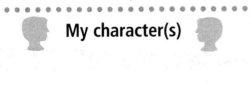

My character(s)

! The problem !

Think of a way to solve the problem.

 Attempt 1

Think of another way to solve the problem.

 Attempt 2

Choose the better way to finally solve the problem. Draw a star ★ beside it.

On another sheet of paper, write a story. Include the character or characters, the problem, and how it was solved.

The Plot Thickens

Stir up your ideas for a story by filling in the shapes below.

Who are your characters?

What is the problem?

Write three or four ways to solve the problem. Include one solution that is "unusual but doable."

1. _____
_____
2. _____
_____
3. _____
_____
4. (This one's unusual!) _____
_____

Choose the best attempt to finally solve the problem. Draw a star beside it.

On a new sheet of paper, write a story. Include the problem, three attempts the character or characters make to solve it, and the solution.

Writing Free-Form Poetry

Skill: *Evoke images and emotions using carefully chosen words.*

Description

Most primary grade children enjoy poetry. They may be familiar with the humorous rhyming poems of Jack Prelutsky and Shel Silverman or non-rhyming poems by Patricia Hubbell and others. Regardless of the subject, poets use carefully chosen words, images, rhythm, and sounds to craft their messages and to evoke emotions. In this chapter, we focus on free-form poems in which questions become poems. The use of free-form poems in the primary grades allows children to play with poetry imaginatively without concern for particular formulas or rhyming schemes.

Getting to Know the Concept

After reading poetry for enjoyment, talk about the writer's word choices and images, the sounds the words create, the grouping of words into lines (line breaks), and the feelings the poems suggest. In *Awakening the Heart* (1999), Georgia Heard talks about different doors through which poets travel to find ideas and words for poems. One door is Heard's "Wonder Door," where writers' questions serve as the source for their poems. We introduce the concept of free-form poetry through the use of the Wonder Door, transforming student questions into poems and building on the curious nature of young children.

Teaching the Concept With Literature

As with all genres, before children can write poetry, they should be exposed to a wide variety of poems and poets. Although it is easier to find poems that rhyme, reading poetry that doesn't rhyme, by poets such as Patricia Hubbell and Kristine O'Connell George, helps children see that an author's message and images—not rhyming patterns—are key to well-written poetry.

Model Lesson

Start by bringing in an array of interesting objects, such as a bird's feather, a piece of driftwood, an old-fashioned pocket watch on a chain, a paint brush with dried paint on it, or an unusual stuffed animal—a puffin, for instance. Let students know that you're going to be brainstorming as many questions as possible about a target object in order to generate a variety of creative and poetic possibilities. Initiate the discussion by posing some of your own open-ended questions for one of the objects—for instance, "What interesting places did the bird's feather visit before it fell out?" Invite children to ask their questions, and jot all questions down on chart paper for the time being.

Then read aloud Patricia Hubble's poems "Elephant at the Zoo" and "Crows" (both are in *Earthmates*, 2000). "Elephant at the Zoo" is a 5-line, 13-word poem that questions why the elephant never changes. After children share what they notice about that poem, read aloud "Crows" and then discuss it. Students may notice, for example, that "Crows" is made up of an 8-word question. Talk about the question, the comparison of the flying crows to a shadow that exploded, the line breaks, and the way the words are arranged.

Return to the questions you and your students posed earlier. Read through the list and select one that's intriguing. Then play with line breaks, grouping the words into a poem of different configurations with perhaps a change or addition of words (Heard, 1999). Read each new version of the poem so students can hear how it sounds. After you and your students have decided on the version you like best, select a different question. Ask pairs of students to transform the question into a poem by grouping the words in different ways on different lines. Some words may need to be replaced by more interesting or precise words. Have pairs create an appropriate title and then share their poems in a large group.

Finally, read aloud "Mystery" from *Little Dog Poems* (George, 1999) and ask children what they notice about the placement of the question in this poem. (The author introduces the topic in the first stanza and then poses the question in the second stanza. Patricia Hubbell does this, too, in "Dandelions," from *Black Earth, Gold Sun*). Model this variation. Have students return to the poems they wrote in pairs and try out this placement. To conclude the lesson, ask pairs to share their poems and then recap key ideas: poems can be created from intriguing questions; poetry doesn't have to rhyme; and poets create images with words, sounds, and line breaks.

Graphic Organizers

When students can pose interesting open-ended questions and use line breaks to separate words, they are ready for one of the graphic organizers. You may want to suggest topics to get students started.

Beginning: **I Wonder . . .**
Students draw a picture to show what they wonder, write a question to go with the picture, and use line breaks to transform the question into a poem.

Developing: **From 3 Questions to a Poem**
Students write three things they wonder, brainstorm a question for each one, check off the question they think will make the best poem, and then use line breaks to transform the question into a poem.

Extending: **Stepping Into Poetry**

Students select a topic and brainstorm ideas they could use to introduce it (first stanza). They write an interesting question about the topic (second stanza). On a new sheet of paper, they use their ideas to create a poem.

Great Books for This Activity

Picture Books

Hubbell, P. (2001). *Black earth, gold sun.* New York: Marshall Cavendish. (See "Dandelions," p. 12; "Grass," p. 14; "Question for a Hollyhock," p. 15; "Cabbage," p. 15; and "Apple Shadows," p. 28.)

Hubble, P. (2000). *Earthmates.* New York: Marshall Cavendish. (See "The Phantom Fawn," p. 5; "Owl," p. 11; and "Turtle Questions," p. 29.)

George, K. O. (1999). *Little dog poems.* New York: Clarion. (See "Coming Home," p. 28; "Present," p. 30; and "Mystery," p. 31.)

Professional Resource

Heard, G. (1999). *Awakening the heart.* Portsmouth, NH: Heinemann.

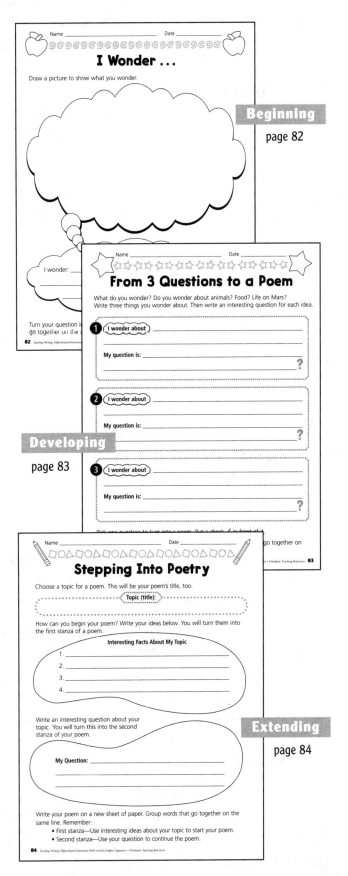

Beginning
page 82

Developing
page 83

Extending
page 84

I Wonder . . .

Draw a picture to show what you wonder.

Write a question to go with your picture.

I wonder: _____

_____

_____

Turn your question into a poem. On a new sheet of paper, group the words that go together on the same line.

From 3 Questions to a Poem

What do you wonder? Do you wonder about animals? Food? Life on Mars?
Write three things you wonder about. Then write an interesting question for each idea.

1 **(I wonder about)** _____

_____

My question is: _____

_____ **?**

2 **(I wonder about)** _____

_____

My question is: _____

_____ **?**

3 **(I wonder about)** _____

_____

My question is: _____

_____ **?**

Pick one question to turn into a poem. Put a check ✓ in front of it.

On a new sheet of paper, write your poem. Group the words that go together on the same line. Give your poem a title. What it is about?

Stepping Into Poetry

Choose a topic for a poem. This will be your poem's title, too.

Topic (title):

How can you begin your poem? Write your ideas below. You will turn them into the first stanza of a poem.

Interesting Facts About My Topic

1. _____
2. _____
3. _____
4. _____

Write an interesting question about your topic. You will turn this into the second stanza of your poem.

My Question: _____

_____

_____

Write your poem on a new sheet of paper. Group words that go together on the same line. Remember:

- First stanza—Use interesting ideas about your topic to start your poem.
- Second stanza—Use your question to continue the poem.

Producing a Book Report

Skill: *Determine the important elements in narrative texts.*

Note: *It's best to teach this lesson after you have worked with students on both Character chapters and the Plot chapter.*

Description

A book report in the primary grades is a summary of a storybook and includes all the important elements of the book that make up the story line. A book report should include all the pieces of story grammar: characters, setting, problem, attempts to solve the problem, and solution. More advanced readers may include the genre, tone, and their opinion of the story. Teaching students to include all these components reinforces important concepts in the story and presents a framework to help ensure that the summary includes all the important pieces of the story.

Getting to Know the Concept

Explain to the class that book reports give other readers a chance to learn what a story is about. If your class is familiar with retellings, you can tell students that book reports and retellings are very similar. To introduce the concept, choose a book that you have read to the class. Without giving the book's title, tell the story to the class. Ask students if they can give you the title of the book. Once they have, ask how they identified the book. Discuss the parts of the story that "gave it away"—such as characters, setting, and plot. Emphasize that all these components are included in book reports. Also talk about the genre of the story (mystery, fantasy, adventure) and its tone, explaining that this is the author's way of portraying the book as funny, serious, or scary. Have students discuss with partners whether they liked the book and explain why.

Teaching the Concept With Literature

Obviously a book report could not exist without literature. At the primary grade level, we need to choose books carefully as we teach children to write book reports. Some of your third-grade students may be able to read *Charlotte's Web* without much difficulty, but writing a book report on such a lengthy story could turn into a frustrating experience or produce an end product with many pieces of the story missing. Help students choose books with an easy-to-identify problem and a limited number of characters.

Model Lesson

Alexander, Who's Not (Do you hear me? I mean it!) Going to Move (Viorst, 1995) is a delightful story with one main problem: Alexander does not want to move, but he will be forced to do so anyway. This story or one that similarly contains a very apparent main problem is a good choice. Begin by reading the book to your students. Use a chart like the one shown below to write a skeleton report by filling in the story components with your students. When the chart is complete, use class input to model writing a report.

When you have finished the model report, discuss the genre of the book (fiction) and its tone (humorous). Have partners discuss whether they liked the book and explain why. Discuss how to rate a book from 1 to 10 to show whether students liked it, then create a section with a simple tally to record students' opinions. Add a short paragraph at the end of the chart including this information.

Graphic Organizers

Once students can identify story elements, they will be ready for one of the following graphic organizers. You may suggest a title, help students choose one, or allow them to make a selection independently.

Beginning: **Picture This Book**
Students write the book title and author and draw the main characters, setting, problem, and solution. Then they give an opinion about the book and write a sentence about each picture.

Developing: **Book It**
Students write the book title and author, draw the main characters in the setting, write the

---

Title and Author: *Alexander, Who's Not (Do you hear me? I mean it!) Going to Move* by Judith Viorst
Main Character(s): Alexander, Mom, Dad, brothers
Setting: house and neighborhood
Problem: Alexander must move with his family. He doesn't want to leave his friends and neighborhood.
Attempts to Solve Problem: Alexander imagines he can live with his neighbors or in a tree house. He thinks maybe his dad is teasing. His brother says he can live in the zoo.
Solution: Alexander decides to move with his family, but says he will never move again.
Genre: Realistic Fiction
Think about how you would rate this book (10 is the best ever!): 1   2   3   4   5   6   ⑦   8   9   10
Tally: Liked: ⊬⊬ ⏐⏐   Didn't Like: ⏐⏐   Not Sure: ⏐

problem, attempts to solve it, and the solution. On a separate sheet of paper, they write a report about the book that includes their opinion.

Extending: **Book Reporter**

Students write the book title and author, the main characters, the problem, attempts to solve it, and the solution. On a separate sheet of paper, they write a report about the book including genre, tone, and their opinion.

Great Books for This Activity

Picture Books

Altman, L. J. (1993). *Amelia's road*. New York: Lee & Low. (This simple story contains well-defined elements.)

Burton, V. L. (1939). *Mike Mulligan and the steam shovel*. New York: Houghton Mifflin. (This old classic has definable story elements.)

Viorst, J. (1995). *Alexander, who's not (Do you hear me? I mean it!) going to move*. New York: Scholastic.

Chapter Book

Dadey, D., & Jones, M. T. (2005). *The abominable snowman doesn't roast marshmallows*. New York: Scholastic. (This story about Bigfoot contains a simple, easy-to-follow plot.)

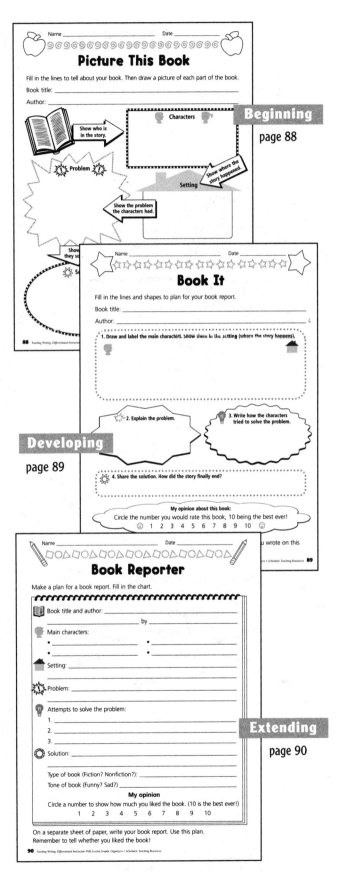

Name _____ Date _____

Picture This Book

Fill in the lines to tell about your book. Then draw a picture of each part of the book.

Book title: _____

Author: _____

Characters

Show who is
in the story.

Problem

Show where the
story happened.

Setting

Show the problem
the characters had.

Show how
they solved it.

☀ **Solution**

My opinion!

Did you like this book?
Circle a face.

yes   no   not sure

On another sheet of paper, write
a sentence about each picture you
drew to tell about your book.

Name _____   Date _____

Book It

Fill in the lines and shapes to plan for your book report.

Book title: _____

Author: _____

1. Draw and label the main characters. Show them in the setting (where the story happens).

 2. Explain the problem.

3. Write how the characters tried to solve the problem.

4. Share the solution. How did the story finally end?

My opinion about this book:
Circle the number you would rate this book, 10 being the best ever!
☹ 1 2 3 4 5 6 7 8 9 10 ☺

On another sheet of paper, write a book report. Use the ideas you wrote on this page. Remember to tell why you did or did not like this book.

Name _____ Date _____

Book Reporter

Make a plan for a book report. Fill in the chart.

Book title and author: _____

_____ by _____

Main characters:

- _____   • _____

- _____   • _____

Setting: _____

_____

Problem: _____

_____

Attempts to solve the problem:

1. _____

2. _____

3. _____

Solution: _____

_____

Type of book (Fiction? Nonfiction?): _____

Tone of book (Funny? Sad?) _____

My opinion

Circle a number to show how much you liked the book. (10 is the best ever!)

1   2   3   4   5   6   7   8   9   10

On a separate sheet of paper, write your book report. Use this plan.
Remember to tell whether you liked the book!

Responding to Literature
(Double-Entry Journals)

Skill: *Use writing to enhance comprehension.*

Description

Often, young readers exert so much energy on decoding that comprehension suffers. In other instances, children read quickly, equating good readers with fast readers, sometimes at the cost of understanding what they've read. One tool that helps primary readers focus on comprehending and learning from their reading is the double-entry journal, or dialectical journal, which is a two-column reading response journal. In the left column, readers record pictures, words, phrases, notes, quotes, or summaries from a book. In the right column, they reflect on each of these entries. By having students keep double-entry journals, they take on the habits of good readers, who continually monitor for comprehension and reflect on what they've read.

Getting to Know the Concept

As teachers, we generally pause at various points during read-alouds with children to discuss key ideas. We elaborate on what's in the text, pose questions readers might ask the author, or help students make connections to something else they've read or to their lives. When we stop periodically to think aloud about what we've read, we are modeling the reflective processes we want children to develop. Many teachers model this process orally at first and then through the use of double-entry journals.

Here, we modify the double-entry journal for students using the Beginning graphic organizer by having them draw rather than write to make the format more developmentally appropriate. At the Developing and Extending levels, we use a traditional double-entry journal format.

Teaching the Concept With Literature

Double-entry journals can be used for all genres: picture books, chapter books, informational texts, and poetry. When children are comfortable stopping and reflecting orally on what they've read, it's time to introduce double-entry journals with a text that is familiar to them. By using a familiar text, students can focus solely on the purpose and process of keeping the journal. We suggest books that contain simple story lines. In the reflections you model for students, you can elaborate, express opinions, make connections, and ask questions.

Model Lesson

Almost any good text can be used to introduce double-entry journals, but for this lesson, we recommend *Mole Music* (McPhail, 1999), the story of a mole who wants to learn how to make beautiful music. The interesting illustrations depict Mole's life in the tunnel as well as the changing environment above his habitat. After reading the book aloud, return to the beginning and think aloud about the illustration on the front cover. You might question why the mole has the large pick beside him while he's playing the violin or note how interesting it is that Mole uses the light from his hard hat to read music in the dark cave. Next, move page by page through the book, varying the reflections you model about the words and illustrations (elaborate, make connections, raise new questions). Once you've modeled several examples, pause and explain to students that stopping to think about the book often helps readers understand and learn more about the story. Also, many readers find it enjoyable and informative to talk about a book with other readers and to write notes in a journal.

Next, show an enlarged copy of "Just Journaling," the Developing graphic organizer (page 95), and select a sentence from the book to write in the first "book" on the left side of the organizer. Ask students to think about what question or new idea the sentence triggered for them. For example, if you copied the two sentences that describe how Mole checked his mailbox every day but didn't find the violin he was expecting, students might suggest the following new ideas: *Mole must have been disappointed. Maybe Mole began to wonder if he would ever get his violin.* Jot down their responses in the "profile" on the right. Return to the book, read a few more pages, select another interesting sentence to record in the organizer, and elicit student responses to fill in the second "profile."

You may initially use just the Beginning and Developing graphic organizer with your students. If you have more advanced students, however, who are able to summarize sections of the text (rather than focus just on individual sentences), you should introduce the Extending graphic organizer. Begin by modeling how to make an entry on the Extending graphic organizer (page 96). Write a summary statement on the left side of the organizer. For instance, you might summarize the first half of *Mole Music* this way: *Mole believes that something is missing in his life, so he buys a violin. He practices and practices. He doesn't know it, but the tree, animals, and people who live above his cave can hear his beautiful music.* On the right side of the organizer, reflect on the summary by jotting down a question or new idea, such as the following: *The people and animals seem to relax and enjoy Mole's music,* or *It must have taken Mole a long time to become good at playing the violin because the tree was small at the beginning of the book but much larger by the middle of the book.* Conclude the lesson by reminding students that writing in double-entry journals may help them think about what they are reading in new and interesting ways. It may also help them recall in the future what they have read.

Graphic Organizers

When students are able to reflect on what they've read by generating new ideas or questions, they are ready for one of the graphic organizers. You may want to steer students to specific books you've been reading in your class or allow them to make their choices independently.

Beginning: **On Second Thought**

Students draw a picture on the left side of the organizer and write a question or new idea in response to their drawing.

Developing: **Just Journaling**

Students jot down a sentence from the book they are reading on the left side of the organizer and record the page number of the excerpt. On the right, they compose a question or new idea that helps them reflect on the sentence.

Extending: **Thinking on Paper**

Students summarize two important sections of the text that make them curious or help them generate new ideas. Then they reflect on their summaries.

Great Books for This Activity

Picture Books

McPhail, D. (1999). *Mole music*. New York: Henry Holt.

Note: All picture and chapter books across genres and content areas are appropriate for double-entry journals.

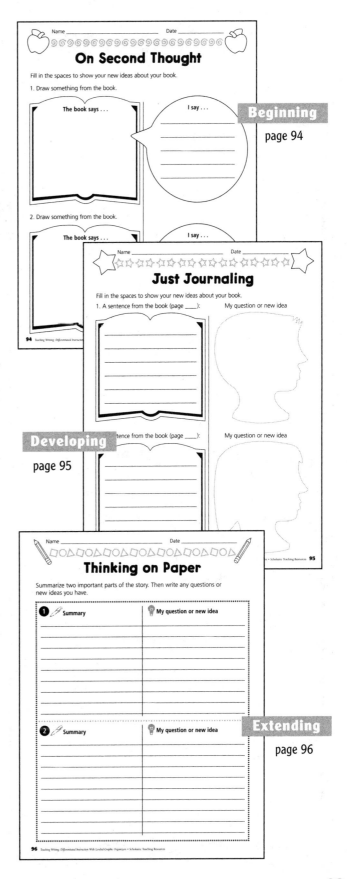

page 94

page 95

page 96

Name _____ Date _____

On Second Thought

Fill in the spaces to show your new ideas about your book.

1. Draw something from the book.

The book says . . .

I say . . .

_____
_____
_____
_____
_____

2. Draw something from the book.

The book says . . .

I say . . .

_____
_____
_____
_____
_____
_____

Name _____ Date _____

Just Journaling

Fill in the spaces to show your new ideas about your book.

1. A sentence from the book (page ____):

My question or new idea

2. A sentence from the book (page ____):

My question or new idea

Thinking on Paper

Summarize two important parts of the story. Then write any questions or new ideas you have.

1 🖊 **Summary**   💡 **My question or new idea**

_____   _____
_____   _____
_____   _____
_____   _____
_____   _____
_____   _____
_____   _____
_____   _____

2 🖊 **Summary**   💡 **My question or new idea**

_____   _____
_____   _____
_____   _____
_____   _____
_____   _____
_____   _____
_____   _____
_____   _____